T0245489

HOW TO RUN AN INDIE LABEL

HOW TO RUN AN INDIE LABEL

Alan McGee

RARE BIRD
LOS ANGELES, CALIFORNIA

This is a genuine Rare Bird Book

Rare Bird Books
6044 North Figueroa Street
Los Angeles, California 90042
rarebirdbooks.com

FIRST NORTH AMERICAN HARDCOVER EDITION

For more information, address:
Rare Bird Books Subsidiary Rights Department
6044 North Figueroa Street
Los Angeles, California 90042

Library of Congress Cataloging-in-Publication Data

Printed in the United States

To all the people who bought the records

CONTENTS

Part Three: The Comedown and Rebirth

INTRODUCTION

....

by John Robb

I've known Alan McGee since 1981. It was the tail end of
the punk rock wars, a time of post-punk DIY ideology and
a belief that we could change the world with three chords
and self-released records. We were all making music on our own
terms, wild-eyed outlaws who believed in the power of rock 'n'
roll. Anything was possible and the music scene was a wild west
full of possibilities and dreams.

It's been a long and strange journey. Whilst some people made
records, others made history.

Some people made both.

Before that, growing up in the pre-punk seventies, no one would
have thought of running a record label, let alone releasing a record.

1

That seemed like a supernova glam world, way out of reach of mad music geeks like Alan McGee. Punk rock changed all that. It was empowering and it tore a hole in the cultural fabric and allowed everyone in.

Looking back, decades later, McGee would say of the mid-nineties Britpop years, 'We all took too many drugs, and my behaviour was quite mad.' In those post-punk years, however, when everything was possible, he took no drugs but was perhaps even madder. In that time of both grinding political nihilism and thrilling cultural possibility, he was like a whirlwind of energy and enthusiasm, driven to make sense of the world and his own life through music. As we all plotted our own take on this brave new world, he suddenly appeared out of the ether. I couldn't say no to the vision from this passionate and fiery Scottish voice crackling down the line when I picked up the phone at my parents' house in Blackpool, where I was living for a few months after being kicked out of Stafford Polytechnic.

I was one of the early people to get the McGee treatment. That tidal wave of spittle-flecked optimism wrapped in a strong Glasgow accent. He was offering my band, the Membranes, a gig in London and would not take no for an answer. We had decided for some long-lost reason that we would never play the capital again. It was the kind of irrational decision that defined the maverick ridiculousness of the then underground music scene as we railed against the then-horrible music-biz stench of the small-gig circuit of the capital. Maybe this was because the gigs in the big city were rubbish – you were treated like fools who were desperate to play in London because, hey, you might get spotted by a label!

Unlike the rest of the country, where there was a spider's web of thriving local scenes appearing on the back of the fanzine culture, with 'zine editors and music fans putting on gigs and building networks in their towns, the London venues made you feel you were lucky to be allowed to play in their city. They thought it was an honour for desperate bands to drive all the way there and back on the same day for the half-hour set that they often wanted you to pay for. The venues had pick-and-mix bills of bands, and came with grumpy promoters who hated the music. For fresh-faced new bands there seemed to be nowhere in the city that was remotely interested.

We had experienced enough of this London gig vibe in joints where there was no sense of community or scene. Of course, we were not superstars, but we were beginning to build a good following after one of our early 1981 releases, 'Muscles', was made single of the week in the music press and played relentlessly by John Peel. We had also just had our first big feature in Sounds music paper, written by Dave McCullough. The late music writer was a firebrand, fixated on the brave new world of post-punk ruckus and like a parallel scribe to the NME's Paul Morley. They were both seeking out the music future with a wild enthusiasm and ornate and captivatingly pretentious prose, armed with an entertaining and compelling vision about what music could be. Dave was

3

tireless, typing his missives whilst sieving through the post-punk underground of never-ending bands and labels and looking for the gold dust of a new direction in the cultural confusion.

Punk had affected people and made them want to do something – anything – and writers like these seemed like lone wolves, typing extraordinary and thrillingly affected missives about obscure skinny outsiders, many of whom have become unlikely gate-crashers in the mainstream.

In 1981, Dave came up to Blackpool to interview us on the prom surrounded by vicious seagulls and even more vicious grockles. He was bemused by the plastic weirdness of the place, which had nothing to do with us.

In the same period, Dave also wrote about a young Glasgow band, The Pastels, and other youthful angular outfits like Alan McGee's own early band, The Laughing Apple. He was searching for the holy grail in the fresh-faced guitar youths who were appearing in the post-post-punk hinterland and joining the dots in this fragmented new culture. He was already on the case with the wonderful bands like the caustic snark genius of The Fall to the highbrow pop of Scritti Politti, or the sound of young Scotland – from Postcard Records to the Fire Engines. He was looking for the next narrative in this brave new world. Maybe me, McGee and Stephen Pastel were brief moments of hope before he found his band when he wrote about The Smiths. Once they had been located, music moved into a new phase.

Yet the mavericks that had signposted this journey were too full of idealism and brimming with pop culture to fade away. Whilst Dave was typing, Alan McGee was plotting, and a new bunch of disparate bands were twitching. McGee was savvy enough to spot this. He had just moved to London from Glasgow and was trying to find a space for his band. He was releasing his own records, booking his own gigs and now running his own tiny gig night, and whether by accident or design, he was tearing up the fabric and creating a new pop art future.

Alan had read the interview with us in Sounds *and that's when the phone calls started, which massively entertained my mother who is Scottish and liked hearing this manic accent down the phone whenever she answered.*

Eventually, in 1983, McGee persuaded us to play his new night at the Adams Arms on Conway Street in central London. Calling his club The Living Room, the weekly gig was built around the coterie of underground bands he was collecting and who were beginning to create a new scene coalescing around his new night and his Communication Blur fanzine.

These were bands like the Nightingales, The Three Johns, his own band, and especially Television Personalities. The latter's vision of a high-octane mix of sixties pop art and punk rock would dominate the Creation narrative, from its twitching small roots to Oasis at Knebworth, and that crush collision of sixties beat and seventies punk was the core of what would become the label's aesthetic. It was this disparate scene of maverick bands playing for the wild-eyed promoter in the tiny upstairs room of a London pub that would construct the foundations of future indie. The smallest of small acorns that would grow into the biggest icons, but somehow it all made sense – these were awkward misfit bands who were not playing anyone's game, and each had their own vision that would eventually catch fire. Like McGee, they were musical nut jobs who were always seeking something else.

Of course, Alan was the maddest of them all. Like all the best visionaries, he believed. In everyone. He himself was a rock 'n' roll star but with no perfect vehicle. His own bands were great but they never cut through and he ironically found stardom and escape in being the conduit for everyone else's dreams.

The Living Room gave us all room to live. The club was a blast and the gig was great. It was rammed with fellow souls and gave us and many other lost souls a step into London.

In the idealistic early eighties, it was the only gig in London where the music heads would turn up and where there was a sense of scene. Also, Alan would pay you properly, with the agreed wedge of money pulled out of his pocket, making him the only person with any business savvy on the scene, as he didn't drop money on the floor or lose it from a ripped plastic bag like the drunken promoters at other venues. He even saved a bit every week for his new venture – an as-yet-unnamed record label. It all sounds fundamental now, but in the London of the times it was rare to be treated properly and it was rare that anyone had any vision.

From that point on, McGee and I became pals. I would hang out with him in London and we would talk of changing the world one record at a time. We would meet people in the warehouse at Rough Trade and liberate lots of the records in their huge storeroom, selling them to cover train fares and food. Rought Trade didn't seem to mind. Maybe it was their way of supporting the waifs and strays who made up the indie underground.

In this post-punk hoedown, McGee planned his new label, which he christened Creation after the sixties psych band. I would write about his early label releases in my Rox fanzine and then in Zig Zag magazine, which I had started writing for. I was intrigued by the look of those early Creation records – the Xerox machine folded sleeves inside plastic bags and the pop-art logo on the labels that matched the off-kilter jangle of the music with its punk-rock art ferocity. You could see and feel the love of decibels and the possibilities of guitar pop. There were great songs like The Pastels' 'I Wonder Why', there were obtuse slogans from The Legend!, and there was the mystery-stained melody from The Revolving Paint Dream.

It was all very much a trip and initially hardly anyone was listening. The records got little attention or radio play, yet McGee didn't blink. He had this evangelistic zeal about him and could make anyone feel ten feet tall with his vision and wild enthusiasm. Unlike most people you met in those days, he didn't seem to have any fear, and he also had absolute certainty. At some point this insane energy was going to blow big. It just needed the right band.

Within a year they had turned up c/o a demo tape and the Glasgow connection that is core to this story.

I first met The Jesus And Mary Chain in The Living Room before they played their debut London show. They were shyly detached yet had a surly cool, and McGee was already sketching out a bigger picture for them that they had no idea about. With a couple of killer tunes already in demo stage on the famous cassette that they had given to Bobby Gillespie in his Glasgow club that he had raved about to Alan, his old school pal, they knew their genius but McGee knew how to amplify it.

I did their first interview when Alan came with them to my flat in Manchester at the back end of 1984. I coaxed the quotes out of the reticent Reid brothers before we went to meet the legendary Manchester-based artist Linder Sterling, who had designed iconic sleeves for Buzzcocks and Magazine, to discuss her doing the sleeve artwork for the band's planned debut single. The meeting feels like a thousand years ago now, in a then-grotty, broken Manchester city centre in an old-school cafe by Manchester's then-ugly bus station. We ended the night watching Lee 'Scratch' Perry in the cavernous Hacienda, where Alan had his first meeting with Tony Wilson.

INTRODUCTION

Soon after this, my band was signed to Creation. McGee had come to see us play Reading University in early 1985, where he was impressed by us kicking over a PA system, and one of our followers raving about the band and also The Doors and leather trousers on their shared car journey back home. McGee promptly rang up, signed us and told us to buy leather trousers, which we could not afford so we had to decline this sartorial masterstroke. He got the Mary Chain to wear them instead and they looked great.

We released our first album, Gift of Life, *on Creation. McGee rightly described it as 'schizophrenic', and it was a crazy piece of work that somehow got to number 2 in the indie charts. It was never going to last and of course we were inevitably going to fall out – we were both mad hatters at the time. The last straw – quite literally – came at a Creation Records night where we had to draw lots for who headlined. Of course, we lost, and we didn't speak for a couple of years until I bumped into him at Reading Festival in the backstage compound where he was buzzing on Es. Typically of McGee, we became firm friends again and have wandered in and out of each other's lives for decades. McGee's music-first journey in culture is like mine – but possibly better paid!*

I know his story inside out, and the best way of telling it is around how to run a record label because Alan, like so many of the punk generation, used the sound and fury of that scene to create something. The beauty of punk was that it provided an escape route if you dared to take it. It empowered and it thrilled. McGee escaped the rainy day Glasgow of his youth to become the last rock-star label boss. There was no manual, and if there had been Alan would have torched it. Headstrong and steeped in music, he followed his muse and created the most unique of record labels that defined indie and charted and changed the music scene. He was a musician who ended up running the show, a visionary with vision and a punk with attitude. But he was the type of person whose vision was not propagated through his own band but through his label. His vision of punk crisscrossed with psychedelia was not propagated though his own band but through his label. That vision which borrowed from Television Personalities, became the nineties music mainstream via Creation – with Oasis ending up as the biggest band in the world – and was forged in the underground of wild outsider nights, tiny venues and unsold records.

Alan learned from scratch how to run a record label – an indie label that defined the word – in a story that goes from DIY Letraset record sleeves, scratchy high-treble guitars as machine guns, and mainly awkward young men, to cocaine, helicopters, supermodels and the biggest band in the world. Despite the seismic shift McGee himself never really changed; even at the stadium height he was still the DIY label boss full of gold dust and ideas and that vibrant enthusiasm.

Somehow, the song had remained the same.

PROLOGUE

·······································

Where it all began

The music biz is nuts and there is space for all kinds of mavericks, but I think we took it to the extreme. We made crazy decisions. Signed lunatic bands and made and lost fortunes, and it was all done on instinct. But it worked. I've lived a rock 'n' roll lifestyle and I've burned myself out and I've come back. Everything the bands did I did ten times more and it eventually broke me. With Creation Records, I made all the mistakes, had all the triumphs and the label became the most successful in the country. And then I got bored.

If you want to know how to run a record label properly, go and buy a manual. If you want to know how to run a record label as a 24/7 music fanatic living in the eye of the high-decibel hurricane and full of the rock 'n' roll lifestyle, then read on.

I grew up in Glasgow in the sixties and seventies and my home life was grim, but it made me. Glasgow was a tough, angry and violent place, with a reputation for being a hard city that drank a lot, which was deserved. Yet its tough outer shell masked a deep warmth, and it was artier than it was letting on, with, I believe, more galleries per capita than any other city in Europe. Glasgow taught you how to survive, how to front people off and how to get street-smart. It was also a city of deep loyalty and it was where I made the most important friendships of my life – friendships that have stayed with me for decades and were the core of Creation. Even though it was a London-based label, Glasgow and all its personality traits were important in Creation Records.

Following my birth in1960, I lived in Govanhill near Paisley, before moving to Mount Florida in 1963. I was just around the corner from Hampden Park, where my dad would take me to see Scotland play England every couple of years. Those huge crowds and the amazing atmosphere was like nothing else I'd experienced and maybe planted something in me that I would try and find in music years later. For my weekly fix of football, I was a Rangers fan, as their ground was only half an hour from where I lived. I never did that sectarianism stuff – I don't even believe in god – but football was tribal in Glasgow and very much part of the culture.

When I was a teenager, my father and me seriously fell out and he would beat me, but when I was a wee child all he beat was panels at work. He was a handsome, strong man, and when I was young seemed heroic but we grew apart. Especially when music came into my life. By then my home life was violent but I thought everyone's home was like that. It probably was where I lived in Glasgow. It was a tough place, and even more violent when mixed with drink and frustration, and there was not much opportunity for escape. I didn't want that kind of life, so for me, music was my way out.

I always wanted to be in music. I started as a fan, then I had a band, but I was never sure if I was good enough to play music. So I ended up running a record label. I was meant to be behind the scenes but somehow I ended up being the boss. And it was like being a rock star. Growing up in Glasgow was a good background for learning how to run a label: one thing I learned from my father was to have no fear. This would be crucial when I ended up in the music biz. I had nothing to lose, so in some respects, I wasn't frightened to fail.

I hated school and hated the teachers. School was a waste of time. It was violent. There were knife fights in the playground! Anyone who tried at school got battered. No wonder that in that kind of world, even at the age of eleven, before punk came along and changed my life, I was fast becoming a music obsessive. I was a fucking geek. Nobody wanted to hang out with me because I was into weird music that wasn't in the charts. The hard lads liked fighting and a few songs, but the weirdoes and geeks were obsessed with music.

I spent all my money on records – that was my escape and my real education. Glam rock was my O levels and punk rock my A levels. Everything I learned about life came from those seven-inch singles and not from school. I had no idea what I was going to do with this knowledge until punk happened. That was the great thing about punk though. You crossed the line from being a fan to being involved.

To this day I have no idea where this love of music comes from. My parents somehow grew up in the sixties without liking any of the great music of that decade, even though they were young enough to be into it. I've never been able to figure that out. Instead of going to all those classic gigs, they stayed in and listened to Tony Christie. For me, though, it was an obsession, and I would skive off school with my mates and listen to records all day.

These mates were a big part of my journey. It was at King's Park Secondary School on Glasgow's south side where I met them. There was Bobby Gillespie, Robert Young and Jim

Beattie, who would eventually go on to form Primal Scream. I was a year above Bobby at school and he lived around the corner from me. When I met him, he was like me – a normal lad and not a rock star. Robert Young was a wee lad but very bolshie, and would also end up in Primal Scream where he was nicknamed Throb. He was the Les Paul-playing rock 'n' roller and heart-throb of the band before he sadly died in 2014.

At first, we were football boys. We just loved football. Then we got obsessed with music. Bobby is my oldest friend and, like all close pals, we have had an on/off friendship for years, and one that is at the core of the Creation story. Punk was the big moment for us, and going through it together made us best friends forever and we shared music and gigs.

In the very early seventies, I needed money to sort my music fix. Even though I was not yet a teenager, I learned all sorts of tricks to make money on the Glasgow streets, and that kind of resourceful savvy was the best education I had for eventually running a business like a record label. My parents had no money for pocket money, so I had to get a job. I also needed that independence from them and the money to spend on music.

So in 1971, I got a job delivering papers with *South Side News* – the local paper. It was one of those newspapers that was mainly paid for with adverts. Every town had them then.

For every paper that I sold for ten pence, I got to keep four pence. For a week I thought that was great; I think I sold 200 papers so made myself eight quid, which was quite good for the eleven-year-old I was then.

By the second week, I'd worked out a scam. If I went down to the depot at half five in the morning I could steal loads of extra papers, then sell them and not give the paper the money and get the full ten pence. That was a buzz – not only did I have the money to feed my music habit, but there was also the thrill of making money. Both things were the start of the music biz for me in a sense, and the core of what later made me good at running a record label. I loved the buzz of grafting to make money and I could see an escape.

My music fix was changing my life. And for the better. I had so much spare cash I wasn't just buying things I liked. I could afford to buy every record that came out because this was the era of the seven-inch single, and they were only about 50p. So I bought virtually everything that came out, whether I knew the song or not, from this record shop in nearby Battlefield in Glasgow. That's how I know bands like Jethro Tull and Uriah Heep, as well as all the glam shit that I loved which was pop perfection.

For most people my age at the time, glam rock was our soundtrack. I was there from the start in 1971 with T. Rex's 'Get It On', which I bought the day it came out and which was the first record that really connected with me. Then I bought Slade's 'Coz I Luv You' and I was away.

At first, I thought albums were for grown-ups and singles were where it was at for teenagers, which is perhaps true in pop culture. Later on, when I got into albums, I borrowed them from the library and taped them at home. That's how I got into The Beatles – by taping their 1973 compilations, the *Red* and the *Blue* albums, from the library. Those two albums were the point at which most of my generation found The Beatles, a couple of years after they had split up.

I didn't buy an album proper until I bought Bowie's *The Rise and Fall of Ziggy Stardust and the Spiders from Mars* just before that in the summer of 1972. It's one of my all-time favourite albums to this day, and Bowie's still probably my strongest musical influence. He was a life-changer, musically and culturally. Along with Bolan and Slade and the other artists of that period, it was glam that made me who I am. It was always there in the background of Creation. I would argue that, in a way, I'm a child of glam more than a child of punk though you can hear glam in punk as well – The Ramones, another of my favourite bands, had that glam thing about them. I then, after that, also came to love the classics, like Bob Dylan and all the sixties stuff.

Pop was generational then, and there really was a generation gap. That stuff about your parents not understanding it was true. Me being really into music was bad enough for my parents, but my Bowie fixation was too much for my father. Especially when I started wearing a bit of make-up (remember this was Glasgow in the seventies). After that, the beatings really started, and they hurt both physically and emotionally. That affected me deeply, and the only positive side probably was that they drove me deeper into music, and then running the label and making a success of it. On the negative side, that also drove me towards a streak of self-destruction and hedonism, and left me with my own nasty streak and a dose of clinical depression that was eventually diagnosed when I was thirty-five. Music, and later on the success and the drugs, were in many ways my self-medication from the beatings and what they did to me, because no one had heard of depression in the seventies. That decade had a dark side and music was the only salvation, yet that dark confrontational side of me which came from Glasgow is probably why I made it in the music business.

By 1974, at the age of fourteen, I was taking the next step from buying records to going to see live bands in Glasgow. At that time I would be at every gig, whether I liked the artist or not: Queen, Santana, The Who, Alex Harvey and Lynyrd Skynyrd. Glasgow was pretty special for gigs – the crowds were famously some of the toughest yet most loyal in the UK, with an atmosphere to match, just like Hampden

Park. In the sixties and seventies, bands like The Kinks went down so well in the city that they recorded their 1967 *Live at Kelvin Hall* album in Glasgow. It was the same with Status Quo and their 1977 release *Live!* They were recorded there because the atmosphere was like nothing else.

Once I had the bug for live gigs I'd go to anything. I was enthralled and totally excited by the whole experience. It's that buzz that drove me all the way through running Creation and, to be honest, still to this day.

One day Bobby Gillespie knocked on my door and asked me to take him to see Thin Lizzy. He was like a wee kid then – he was only fourteen and I was the grand old age of fifteen. We were already friends but this was the start of a long on-and-off musical journey that we have been on ever since. You see us in the media or in films and they make it look like I'm the Svengali and he was the swaggering rock star, but we are nothing like that. We were both fucking music geeks back then, and we are both music geeks now. He just followed his music obsession to become a rock star, and I followed mine to create and run a label. We were driven and we were fans and that's the truth.

Running a record label is not something you plan to do when you get into music. Especially not in Glasgow, as the music biz seemed like something that went on somewhere else, like London, which felt totally remote from us. I was just into the bands and the music, and I didn't have a plan beyond that – but my time spent growing up in the city certainly helped put me on the road to running a record label attitude-wise, even if I had to go to London to do it.

Everyone has self-doubt, but failing with Creation was never an option. Fear of failure was the reason for my inner confidence – that's what drove me. I couldn't go back. The determination not to end up with the lives my parents had or what was laid out in front of me in Glasgow was a driving force for me in running a record label – and is crucial for anyone who is creative. I had to make the label work. The only place for me was in music.

I was not your typical record label boss either. I had the vision and belief, a kamikaze attitude to business, and I was totally immersed in it. Creation became the biggest indie label of them all and the records we released were the soundtrack to the nineties, but when I started out it was a DIY operation. That was not by choice, but it was a brilliant education. I didn't know how you ran a record label, but it made sense at the time and I made it up as I went along. At first, we would stick our own sleeves together and try to get the press and radio interested in the singles. I signed bands on instinct and belief. I also signed bands not just because of the music; often it was because I was intrigued with the people in them. I believed in them. Some became massive and some disappeared. I must have been totally mad but I was driven by self-belief and a passion for music and music culture.

I learned all this from the streets of Glasgow and from my love of records and gigs. I knew that music was going to be my life, but I had no idea how. I was an outsider and I didn't have any way in, and then punk happened...

PART ONE

Getting Started

CHAPTER 1

....

A DIY attitude can make things happen

Growing up in Glasgow, you never met anyone who was in a band, let alone ran a record label. Even a mad wee music nut like me, who bought every record he could, had no idea he could cross over to the other side. Punk was the revolution that made me and other kids believe that we could do it. Anyone my age will tell you the same. We were the right age at the right time with the right attitude for the right music. Punk changed our lives – it lit a fire that's never gone out.

In many ways, I was a ticking time bomb and perfectly primed for punk. In 1977, in the middle of my darkest times,

I heard the Sex Pistols' 'God Save The Queen' and it was a life-changing moment. Looking back now, I obviously had depression, but it was undiagnosed because no one knew what it was back then. In those days, all people would say was 'pull yourself together' – if you even mentioned it, which you never would. My father's bullying fucked me up and made me angry and alienated, a cynical crazy bastard, which was perfect for punk and then for the music biz, and so I have to thank him for that. The way I grew up made me want to make something of myself, to escape, and punk was the perfect catalyst. It arrived at just the right time to fire up teenage minds like mine, taking the dreams of glam and making them a reality. I left school in 1977 with only one O level, but now the music was my education and my life.

Punk was like all the best bits of previous pop culture cut up and put back together into something far more incendiary and exciting. It was all-consuming and its simplicity made it easy to get into. It didn't just create a great soundtrack; there was an urgency to it that told you that you had to be part of it as well – here's three chords, now form a band, as Sideburn #1 fanzine famously printed in 1976. If not that, then run a record label or put gigs on or print a fanzine. And if you didn't know what you were doing, who cared? Punk was about empowerment and doing things anyway. Just for the hell of it.

Sex Pistols were the band, and 'God Save The Queen' blew my mind. I didn't really get the politics, or what it was all about at first, but I could feel it and the sound of it really connected with me and the state I was in at the time. I needed more of this new fix so I rushed down to the record shop and bought The Stranglers' 'Go Buddy Go' and The Ramones' 'Sheena Is a Punk Rocker,' and those records were also life-changing for me. All of them. I also loved the possibilities of bands like The Slits or Siouxsie and the Banshees, whose first two albums, *The Scream* and *Join Hands*, still sound amazing. To this day, the people that impress me the most are those from the punk era, like Paul Weller, Siouxsie and John Lydon. I was a total fan. I loved the music, the attitude and the way it made you want to do your own stuff. Glam was great but you couldn't take part in it. All you could do was buy the records. With punk you believed you could be in a band, you could be on *Top of the Pops*, you could be Marc Bolan or David Bowie. No one had believed in you before. You hadn't believed in yourself. Yet punk inspired you. It had a DIY attitude. It said you didn't need anyone's permission to create stuff. And it was a big part of how I ended up running a record label.

For my dad, already pissed off that I was into glam and David Bowie, punk was a step too far. I was obsessed, dressing like a Buzzcock in their modish pop art take on punk, and would put the eyeliner on when I went out. He hated that, and the beatings increased. Punk did that. It was the revolution of the every day. It was a big fuck you.

Eventually, the tension and the beatings got too much and I moved out to a bedsit in Glasgow's West End. It was a crummy place, but at least I was safe. I bought a bass because I was struggling to learn how to play the guitar. I think the bass was the instrument of choice in punk rock because you could learn it pretty quick, and the cool one in most bands seemed to be the bass player. With a bit of messing around, I could blag being a bassist. That was DIY in action. You didn't need to go to music school to be in a band. You just did it. That attitude was crucial to the whole story.

It wasn't long before I found my way in to this new band world. There was a punk show on the local station Radio Clyde every Wednesday night hosted by Brian Ford. A show like that was pretty rare at the time as most radio stations would not play punk. They were scared of it, which made it even better. On the show there was an advert for a band called The Drains, who were looking for a bass player. I answered the ad and that's how I met Andrew Innes, who would end up being part of the core of Primal Scream. It was his bedroom band with his next-door neighbour, Pete Buchanan, on drums. Innes was the guitar player. I thought it was a shit name for a band but it was probably just Andrew taking the piss out of shit band names with his sarky sense of humour. In the grand tradition of punk rock, Innes taught me to play bass as we sat in his bedroom. It didn't matter that I couldn't play when I turned up. This was about learning on the job. Picking out the riffs as you went. Innes would put my fingers on the correct frets and I would fumble and try to play along. It was just like Paul Simonon when he joined The Clash, with Mick Jones teaching him how to play. That was how punk worked. You just got on with it. There were no barriers.

A couple of hours of fumbling with the bass and we had a band. It wasn't long before Bobby Gillespie would tag along to our Friday night sessions as well. Even though we were just playing in a bedroom it felt like the real deal to us. For a wee while, as we did The Drains, we also had these imaginary bands in our heads, like the jokingly named Captain Scarlet and the Mysterons. We were just messing around, but we were also serious in trying to make something happen even then. We would start by singing The Clash, Sex Pistols and even Sham 69 songs in Andrew's bedroom whilst he worked out the chords because he was by far the most musical out of us all. We were getting our kicks on these nights when there were no punk gigs to go to, which, to be honest, was most nights.

Innes could really play, though. That was really something at the time because in those days no one learned guitar. No one at school even had a guitar! It seemed amazing that he knew all this stuff. We would spend all night learning and eventually we could perform the whole of the first Clash album that had come out in April 1977. By then Bobby would be singing and also rolling around on the floor doing his Iggy Pop thing – although, thinking about it, it was more likely to have been his Jimmy Pursey thing because he was a big fan of Sham 69 then – whilst us older guys drank beer and played the bass and guitar.

By 1978 we had renamed ourselves Newspeak after George Orwell's *1984*, which I had just read, got a good-looking lad called Jack Riley in on vocals, and added Neil Clark, who ended up being the guitar player in Lloyd Cole and the Commotions after Newspeak. I guess this was what everyone was going through at the time – trying out bands in the hope of finding something that worked and like-minded people to work with. It was a revolving door of young kids fired up by punk running around the city looking for bands to be in.

About the same time, Innes and I also started playing in a local band called H2O. They were a new wave band who went on to have a couple of hits after I left. I played bass with them for about four months and got Innes in for a short stretch as well, playing guitar. H2O wasn't punk rock but it was cool to be in a proper band and they were good guys. They taught us a lot about music and being in a real band rather than a bedroom punk band. I learned about rehearsing properly and getting organised as a band, which was an early lesson for me in how to run that side of things and already interested me. I still had this raging ambition and desire to escape, driven by my upbringing. That drive to be successful is key in business. To be successful at anything, you have to have willpower. That's more important than having talent, and is especially true in the music business, even for those independent labels that liked to look like they were above that kind of thing. We were all the same.

People in the city remember me as being on the fringes of the Glasgow scene at the time. In Glasgow I wasn't even in the fucking top 200 people most likely to make it in the city! I was on the outside of the outside. People in the local music scene thought that my band were the 27th most likely to make it. Out of 30. That's how much of an insider I was.

I felt that I had come from nowhere. And it looked like I was staying there. Newspeak were playing gigs and starting to sound good though. I had sent demos out to record labels looking for a deal but no one replied. Yet being in the band gave me hope. By then I had got a job at British Rail, but being in the band was getting me through. I didn't really have any big plans apart from some idea of escape, and maybe I would still be in Glasgow in the 27th most likely band to make it if my life hadn't suddenly been uprooted and changed.

It was Innes's idea to move the band to London. He figured that if we were serious about what we were doing, then we would have to make the big move. I would not have had the balls to go to London if I had not been persuaded to go there by Innes. I had all the arguments about why we shouldn't go because life had got good for me in Glasgow. Finally, at the age of nineteen I was in a good place: I had left home and had just got my first proper girlfriend, Yvonne, who I would eventually marry, and the band was doing ok. With all this I wanted to stay in Glasgow, but Innes won the argument.

If you are serious about anything, whether it's being in a band or running a record label, you have to give it your all and leave your old life behind. You may not have to move cities in the internet age but you can't do this kind of thing as a hobby. You have to be in it 24/7 and have no safety net. Mind you, I was never really a safety net kind of guy. So in 1980 me and Andrew made a few trips down to London, sort of scouting it out before we decided to make the big move. As the Small Faces sang, 'It's All or Nothing'. To run a record label or make an impact with anything, you have to take chances. You have to be prepared to rip it up and start again.

Change your life, change your hair or change your city... At the time the last option was the easiest. And it wasn't easy.

Innes had the vision. He realised that the music business was not interested in Glasgow. In the late seventies, Glasgow was not the place that it is now. Today, it's a culturally fast-forward city with a brilliant music scene, a place that young musicians and creatives stay in and also move to. But back then that was a totally alien concept – most of the northern English and Scottish cities were on their arses. It wasn't so much where you were from or where you were at, it was about where you moved to. London seemed like the punk Mecca. There were mini-punk scenes in other cities, like Manchester, but they were tiny. London was where all the action was. And we wanted to be there.

We didn't have a plan. I grabbed a small bag of clothes and my new Yamaha bass, and with a head full of dreams I went with Innes down south to London to become a pop star. Jack Riley came with us and we moved to a tiny bedsit in Tooting. To mark the big change we renamed Newspeak, The Laughing Apple. We were broke and back at the bottom and in a strange new city, but there was a thrill to it. Suddenly the speed of the blood in our veins was faster. We had the in and the info on the big city. Everyone in Glasgow thought that we were on the inside of the music biz, even though we were penniless and living in a squat. The minute we moved we were six months ahead of everyone in Glasgow, despite us being on the outside of the scene in London.

It was the right move, of course. If I had stayed in Glasgow and not listened to Innes I would never have started Creation and none of this would have happened. I would still be in Glasgow. Going nowhere. Sometimes you just have to take chances and start all over again. I've done that several times in my career, though maybe nothing as dramatic as that first big move. Punk and its DIY ethos provided the perfect inspiration for breaking out of the shackles and creating a brave new world to run amok in.

Living in London without much money was a new kind of tension and Jack didn't last long. Me and Innes picked on him all the time – he was the band scapegoat. Jack was a nice lad from a nice background and Innes was a sarcastic Glasgow guy and I was fucked up and full of anger from my background. It didn't take long for us to wear him down and he had enough and went back to Glasgow and Innes took over the vocals in the band.

Moving to London was pivotal, but living there when we first moved down was tough. The streets were certainly not paved with gold and we saw a lot of those streets as we went from one bedsit to another and from one squat to another. It was an endless series of these squats and shared houses full of mad fuckers and lost heroin addicts. It seemed like the people around us were all taking drugs, which, ironically, we had no interest in at the time. It seems hard to believe now but me and Innes had never done any drugs at this point. There had been no drugs in our scene back in Glasgow. Same with Bobby. We were so young and so naive. It was hard enough trying to survive in London without throwing drugs into the equation.

Being around that scene and the smackheads in shit damp rooms was a powerful lesson for me and put me off that drug for life. I've probably done nearly every other drug, but that squat heroin world had zero glamour and fortunately didn't interest me at all.

I was bouncing around London from one dead-end place to another, but at least I was in the big city and it gave me a chance. The band were the same, playing one small gig to the next. From the Stockwell Arms to punk dives in Tooting Bec, it was just whatever we could find. This never seemed to dent my drive though. I had to make the band work as I didn't want the mundane nine to five existence. And I didn't want to go back to Glasgow as a failure. I was prepared to put up with a whole heap of shit to avoid that. That drive is the same drive that made Creation work. I wouldn't take 'no' for an answer. That's the big difference between having an idea and finishing it off. That drive was key and it's never left me.

In those early penniless days of being in London I quickly learned how to make things happen. I would hustle gigs, like getting us a support slot at the Moonlight Club in Hampstead, which was one of the best gigs you could get at the time. I went on and on at the promoter until he booked us a support with Scars, who were this brilliant post-punk band from Edinburgh and for that brief period of time the coolest band on the planet. It was our highest-profile gig at the time and I got that by sheer graft and hustling.

I was learning the ropes. Fast. Pretty soon I realised that the band was going to have to do more than just play gigs around London. If we were going to get up the ladder, we would need to get a record out. Luckily for us we were in a period where lots of bands who couldn't get record deals were releasing their own singles on their own labels. I had done the rounds with our demo and it wasn't getting anywhere. We figured that, if no one else was going to sign us, then we needed to make our own singles.

Before punk it would have been impossible for the likes of us to release records, but the fertile space of the DIY indie label scene was a game-changer. It was our 'in'. We already knew about this world after Innes and I had come down from Glasgow to London with our Newspeak demo. Before we moved, we had made the long journey down and taken our demo around places and we'd been rejected. Eventually, after everyone we could think of had rejected us, we took the demo to the Rough Trade shop in west London because we had read about it being the centre of indie DIY. The owner, Geoff Travis, was behind the counter. He looked different from the people we knew in Glasgow. He had big curly hair and looked like Art Garfunkel with a hint of Leo Sayer for his sins. He was from a hippy squat background and that seemed like another world to us. Not like the kind of squats we were in! We were just boys down from Glasgow and not part of that world, yet he gave us time. He was a somebody who actually gave us nobodies a listen, and I have always remembered that.

The next time we went to see him we took The Laughing Apple demo with us. He stunned us by saying that he would take fifty singles for the shop if we self-released it. It seemed amazing and unbelievable to us that someone would be that interested. We just had to find out what he meant by self-release. Once we worked that out, we knew that if we pressed the single we actually had some sales, which was crucial. That off-the-cuff order from Geoff Travis was the first record I ever sold. It was the start of a journey that ended up with Oasis and the biggest band in the world. It also taught me to stay connected with new bands and to trust your instinct on young bands.

With fifty sales promised, I started Autonomy Records in June 1980 to release The Laughing Apple's debut single.

We had previously sent thirty-five demo cassettes of Newspeak to the bigger labels and been ignored, so I set up my own label to release the new seven-inch single. I had stumbled into setting up a record label by chance, yet I would learn so much from putting out those early singles by the band before I had even started Creation. It taught me the basics of how to make records and how to release them. How to press them up and how to make the artwork and how to get them written about or played on the radio.

To get that first single out we saved up our own money and then blagged some extra from the CND of all places to get the £500 that it cost in 1980 to record four tracks back home at Sirocco Studios in Kilmarnock. In 1981 we pressed a thousand copies of our first release, 'The Ha Ha Hee Hee! EP'. We then had to design and print the sleeves. Luckily for us, Bobby Gillespie was, at the time, working at a printers in Glasgow and knew how to design and get the sleeves sent down to London. We pressed the records with a company that we found called Mayking, who were based in London, and then we got Rough Trade to distribute them, starting with that order of fifty copies. It was the kind of low-budget indie that was going on in hundreds of bedsits across the UK. Once we had pressed the singles we sent them to Rough Trade in the post and waited.

Rough Trade were in it for the wee guys like us and that really meant something. They were brilliant. They had such a great system for getting the records out to people. They had set up this distribution network called the Cartel, where alternative record shops all over the country could order records from them. They created this whole thing to get all this DIY music that was getting made out to people. It was a revolutionary time for music because it opened the floodgates; without people like Geoff Travis and Rough Trade, none of the indie music that became huge over the years would have happened. Amazing. The indie scene was booming because of people like them. All over the UK labels were springing up because they had the music to release and because there was the distribution to get it out there. Because of this, people like me were learning about the music business and how to make records.

Some of these new labels would disappear, and some would become the key players in the next few decades, like Factory in Manchester and Mute in London. The primary influence on me, though, was Television Personalities' Whaam! Records label. It was run by the band members Dan Treacy, Edward Ball and Joe Foster, and it showed me that we could have our own label.

Like most post-punk bands, it was early days for these new labels and we were all just guessing. Fumbling in the dark. It was wee nobodies like me taking a chance. At that point I don't think anyone recognised the potential in me because it was too early. I don't even think I saw the me in me at that point either! It was people like Simon Edwards, who worked at Rough Trade along with Geoff Travis, who was the first one to actually recognise something in me. He clocked my enthusiasm, saw this young guy who really believed in the music, and encouraged me to run my label. That kind of empowerment, from people already in the business, was crucial to me in eventually running an indie label.

As I put out those early singles of my own band I would continue to go down to Rough Trade's warehouse near King's Cross. It was a large space full of records that they were distributing. It was like being inside the music business, but full of cool records on the new indie labels that were springing up. I was blagging records and hanging around and was more of a nuisance to them, I guess. We were so skint that we would nick records from the Rough Trade warehouse and sell them in second-hand record shops. They must have known what we were up to and yet they still turned a blind eye, maybe because they were helping us survive. Maybe it was their way of funding people like us. When I look back on this I can see what a revolution it was. The idea that young people like me, who were full of ideas and enthusiasm, had a chance to release our own music was pretty special. That opportunity was the spark and the start for what would become Creation Records.

I was young and I made every mistake but I also picked up knowledge. Just by releasing my own singles and hanging around Rough Trade, I was learning as I went along. I was getting information on how to make and self-release records and how to get them heard. I was doing it the hard way but at least I was getting the information. It helped me go from being a musician, self-releasing my own band DIY-style, to actually learning what a record label does. And I realised at a certain point that not only had I learned what to do but I was also pretty good at it. Somehow, I had picked up all the skills to form an independent record company, from the recording to the pressing, from the distribution to the media. You couldn't get that from a book. You had to do it. Of course, it was real hand-to-mouth stuff, but that was very much in the spirit of the times. Like loads of people at the time, we were blagging it as we went along. Before punk, you had to get on your knees and beg to get a record deal. Now you made your own culture and this made you resourceful and creatively free.

Post-punk DIY was a crash course in creativity. It made people like me get up and do stuff. It was not just being in a band or going to gigs or collecting records. It was also starting magazines, running clubs, putting on gigs and setting up record labels, and I would do all those things. Pretty soon I could manufacture and, with the help of Bobby, create the sleeve design. I then learned to master and produce records and to press records. I'd then take them to radio stations and the music press. I was only twenty but I learned all of this with that first label I created. I also learned how to manage the band, and how that was similar to running a record company.

The Laughing Apple had released three singles when I wondered if I could apply what I had learned to another band, releasing them on a new label. In essence, I already knew how to do it despite being really young. I might have been unwise as a person but I was not unwise as to how to put a record out and get it played on the radio, or get a key music writer to write about the band. Already it felt like maybe I was better at being a manager, a hustler and an organiser than actually being in a band. That learning curve, which I got from Rough Trade, was a genius thing. To this day I respect Geoff Travis and also Richard Scott, who were the architects of the idea of national independent distribution, which was so important. I kinda learned how to do it by being around people like that. I also learned by watching bands like Scritti Politti, Orange Juice and Killing Joke, who all had their records coming through Rough Trade and were becoming big. I watched how they did it and inherently picked stuff up.

* * *

What was unusual about me at that point – apart from being enthusiastic, which was rare in the music biz which could get so jaded – was that I actually had experience of both sides of the business: I had the knowledge from being immersed in music for years, and also first-hand experience of the practical side. And I was a fast learner. By 1981 The Laughing Apple lineup had changed as Andrew had gone back to Glasgow to convalesce, having lost a kidney after contracting hepatitis B. Ken Popple had moved to London and answered our *Melody Maker* ad for a drummer, and his best friend Dick Green soon joined him on guitar; his Will Sergeant style sounded great on the songs. He was from Boston and had been in home town bands, and he would often sit in on rehearsals and sometimes play with us. And when Andrew got ill he joined the band and did a few gigs.

With Andrew now back in Glasgow – where, ironically, he then got a degree in pharmaceuticals at college – the responsibility for the band totally fell on my shoulders, and I soon realised that this was the bit of being in a band that I enjoyed the most. I was hustling press and got a two-page spread in *Sounds* from Dave McCullough. I got Janice Long and John Peel to play our music on their shows. Most people in bands hate having to hustle, but I got really excited by it and Andrew was astonished by the amount of press I was getting for the band and kept telling me I should be a manager instead.

What changed everything was doing a disastrous tour supporting a band called Eyeless In Gaza. My bass got nicked and we crashed our van on the way back from Scotland after Dick, who was driving, hit some black ice. It was all pretty bad, so we knocked the band on the head for a short time. Finally I had the time to do other stuff and could go full-on with a label, so decided to set up Creation, although I had not given up with the idea of being in a band. Dick and I kept in touch as we had become firm friends, and he would eventually become a key part of the Creation story.

I was already branching out. Inspired by the idea that art could be in everything you did, I started the Communication Club in October 1982. Armed with a cheap vocal PA that we had bought, I put gigs on in the back room of a pub in Camden. There was a new crop of bands coming through, like the Nightingales, Television Personalities, The Go-Betweens, The Membranes and Eyeless In Gaza. Of course, at first, no one came. No one seemed to go to gigs in those days, but I was not daunted.

I then got the weekly Living Room gig going in 1983 in the back room of the Adams Arms pub on Conway Street in central London. I called it The Living Room because it was the size of a living room. It was tiny. We put on the Nightingales and the place was rammed – suddenly, it seemed like there was a scene after all. We moved around London as the rooms got busier, to venues like Alice In Wonderland near King's

Cross. I remember The Membranes would show up to play a gig and say the venue has got even smaller, just like in *Alice in Wonderland*, how are you going to fit all the people in?

To begin with, the scene was very DIY – it was me and Dick Green on the door, with Joe Foster from Television Personalities helping out. When Joe arrived at The Living Room he said I owed him a taxi fare for turning up from Hendon, which was a lot of money at that time! I liked his mad attitude and he became part of the inner core of what I was doing. Joe knew his music and he educated me. It was him that got me into the Velvets.

The Living Room was a great platform for the ideas I had about music, and a scene started to coalesce. I was putting on the same bands that I had promoted at the Communication Club, and bands like The Three Johns were now coming to play as well. It was not just about my own music and my own band anymore, I genuinely loved all these bands in every way and thought we shared some sort of vision. The Living Room was really important because it taught me how to deal with bands directly, and helped me to understand and empathise with other bands and how they worked.

It also meant that I made money that I could put into this new label I was putting together. It was going to be called Creation, which would continue the vision I had with the club and with the idea of pop art. Being from a band myself gave me an edge over other labels and managers – I knew the language that the bands understood, and added to this I also knew about the music from my Glasgow years of buying every record that came out. It was the perfect grounding on how to run a record label. All I needed now were some bands to sign.

The Living Room scene itself was not rock 'n' roll – it was pretty wholesome at the time. That stuff came years later, at my Death Disco night, which ran from 2000 to 2009 in London and was carnage, full of celebrities, drink and drugs. That kind of thing didn't happen in the early eighties – the most rock 'n' roll it got then was Stephen Pastel deciding to walk off stage because his amp wasn't working. His band, The Pastels, were one of the first bands I signed. I listened to them recently and their music has stood the test of time. These bands were punk rock, not rock 'n' roll. People were not into that sort of stuff then. The madness came later.

Through The Living Room I made friends with people like The Three Johns, The Membranes, the Nightingales, The Loft, Nikki Sudden, The Jazz Butcher, and upcoming music journalists. When Primal Scream had just formed, they came down to London and played their first show there in August 1993, although Bobby denies it now. It may have been a really early, unformed version at the time, with just Bobby and guitarist Jim Beattie, who showed up with a drum machine to play the drum parts. I don't think Bobby looks on that early lineup as Primal Scream now, but it was on that day though or whatever he christened it.

The music vision of The Living Room and then Creation Records all came from Dan Treacy of Television Personalities. As I've mentioned, that band had a big effect on me. I first saw them in 1982 supporting the Nightingales in London. The gig was amazing. Not only did they sound great but they had this pop art thing going on. It was the gig where Joe Foster sawed Dan Treacy's Rickenbacker guitar in half. It was total art madness, and even more powerful was the fact that the guitar must have been worth a grand and they were only getting paid about £50 for the gig. I was really affected by the performance and the band's vision and loved that sixties punk psychedelic thing that they were doing. I also loved the pop art of the record label Whaam! that Dan Treacy ran with band members Ed Ball and Joe Foster. Being a fan of something, you try and echo it, and I undeniably tried to copy what they were doing, though it inevitably comes out as your own thing. So of course, Whaam! was a major influence on Creation Records. In fact one of the first ever releases on Creation Artifact, which is what the label was called at the start, was a flexidisc distributed with the second issue of my Communication Blur fanzine, which featured two tracks by the Television Personalities.

I'm still a big fan of Dan Treacy to this day. I don't think he gets the proper credit for his influence. He's like a Syd Barrett for our generation, in that he's not known to a big audience but his reach is huge. His vision runs right through Creation. I can draw a line from Television Personalities to Oasis. Ultimately, their punk psychedelic rock 'n' roll is the same as you see in Oasis. That's the way I look at it. It was all started by them, then formulated in The Living Room, and ended up at Knebworth.

What helped me make sense of all this was the Communication Blur fanzine that I had started in 1982. The fanzine actually came before The Living Room; it was steeped in pop art as well, and allowed me to hone the idea of what I was doing and create the vision, attitude and ideals for the Creation label. There was always a manifesto to what you were doing, whether it was a band or a label, and the fanzine helped me to get an idea of mine. Initially, I had a vision of creating a magazine or fanzine to explain my ideas. People may have got them or they may have thought, 'That McGee, he's fucking mad but at least he believes in it.' I started out by printing 500 copies and sold them by hand out of a plastic carrier bag at gigs – the classic fanzine style of distribution.

I started the fanzine with a guy called Jerry Thackray, who would turn up at loads of gigs in London at the time and would eventually become Everett True, the music journalist.

At the time he was this character who was really into his music and would turn up at The Laughing Apple gigs and dance around on his own. We soon nicknamed him 'The Legend' because when we made him the club compere we called him 'the legendary Jerry Thackray' because – in the best possible way – he was the kindest, shyest, most unenigmatic, non-rock 'n' roll person you could ever meet, and it just appealed to my sense of humour to make him compere. So he became The Legend because, ironically, he was quite the opposite. And he ended up doing his own fanzine with the same name and writing for the music press, initially as The Legend.

There was a big fanzine culture at the time – there were post-punk fanzines like Jerry's, and Rox, and the future editor of *Loaded*, James Brown, was also doing one called Attack On Bzag. There were loads of them. All these dudes running around with plastic bags full of zines, empowered by punk, old typewriters and Xerox machines!

I was also influenced by the glossy zines like Tony Fletcher's Jamming!, which was part-financed by Paul Weller. When I was really down and nothing was working, it was Tony Fletcher who inspired me to get going again when, in an issue of Jamming, he restated the punk manifesto of get up off your arse, make a fanzine, form a club, form a band. So I went and did all three.

All this stuff going on – the label, the club night, the fanzine – was perhaps a result of me proving to myself as much as to anybody else what you could do if you put your mind to it. It was me subconsciously working out just what my vision actually was. Typing it out and writing it in the fanzine really shaped that, then the club put it into action, and the label was the result. People used to think I was this crazy guy from Glasgow, and on some level I was, but I was also business savvy, unlike most people on the scene. Decades later I'm still my own boss and I've not had a real job for forty years, so I couldn't have been that shit at it!

I was so into the idea of the sixties and punk thing mixed together that I named the new label after the groundbreaking sixties pop art band The Creation, who I was a big fan of. Their mix of sixties beat, punk rock, feedback, drones and psychedelia was where I was at and provided a musical and pop art template that I would update to the label. The Creation were a really cool band and the first to use a violin bow on a guitar before Jimmy Page. Their 'Making Time' song is a classic. They also wrote 'Painter Man' which Boney M., of all people, turned into a hit, and another song called 'Biff Bang Pow', which was the name of the new band I had just put together with me and Dick Green, with Joe Foster from Television Personalities on bass and Ken Popple on drums.

The weekly gig nights I was putting on in 1983 were going really well. Something had changed out there and the nights were selling out. The Living Room seemed to be where the fringes of the various mini-scenes in London crossed over – the garage rock fans, the mods and the punks, and the post-punk and indie fans. The bands I was putting on were not even on the radar of the bigger promoters like John Curd, but people were going to see them and I was the conduit for it all.

The fanzine was also making its mark, so the next logical step was to get the new label off the ground properly. In 1983 I went back to Rough Trade, and they agreed to front the production and distribution. For the early releases, I was paying for the other costs, whilst Bobby Gillespie designed the sleeves. He made these cool fold-up sheets that were cheaper than proper record sleeve bags, and in the pop art style. We put them in see-through plastic bags like the Fire Engines had done with their brilliant 1981 'Candyskin' single, and we instantly made an impact in the music press. That was pop art – you needed the art aesthetic as much as the music; the two had to work together.

Those first releases on Creation were all seven-inch singles that reflected The Living Room style of bands and the DIY nature of the scene. They are each imprinted on my mind to this day. We started with The Legend's '73 in 83', which was very lo-fi DIY, then the second was Andrew Innes's new band, The Revolving Paint Dream, and their debut 'Flowers in the Sky', which was perfect modern psychedelia. Then I released my new band Biff Bang Pow!'s debut single 'Fifty Years of Fun', followed by the debut single from a new band from Aberdeen I was really into called The Jasmine Minks, then my fellow Glasgow band The Pastels' single 'Something Going On', before the psychobilly garage of The X Men, and then another Biff Bang Pow! single and the second single from The Jasmine Minks, 'Where The Traffic Goes'. Then in 1984 I released the debut single by a great new band called The Loft. Their 'Why Does the Rain?' captured something quite special, with a crafting of the classics like Television but filtered through the post-punk world we were living in. They had given me a demo because, at the time, their band was initially also called The Living Room. I guess someone thought we must have something in common. It took me a while to totally get them, but there was something in there so I kept giving them support slots at my nights. When it was released 'Why Does the Rain?' was the first record I put out that started to take off, and it was getting played by Janice Long on the radio. It was also the first to sell all 1,000 copies that we had pressed up, and the first band that felt successful in our underground indie world. I was running around London bigging everything up to the press and radio, and I think the music writers dreaded this crazy ginger-headed Scot with this mad Glaswegian accent haranguing them, but it seemed like people were listening and The Loft was our first minor breakout. We then released another single from The Legend, and then The Pastels, and then it all went crazy with our twelfth release, The Jesus And Mary Chain's debut single 'Upside Down' in November 1984. At that point all our ambition and my outrageous blagging for the label caught fire and we actually had a hit record.

Things were never the same after that. Now people had to listen to me and the label. Up to that point, I think people must have thought that McGee was this entertaining character, running in and out of the Carnaby Street pubs with whoever, trying to get writers interested in the bands I was releasing. The music press obviously thought I was a bit of a freak because instead of banging on about Hipsway and the big Scottish bands of the time, there was this wee guy going on about these new underground bands playing this mad guitar music on his label. I suspect they thought I was so unusual that, just maybe, it might work. The writers also wanted their own scene that they could write about – maybe they felt that they had missed punk and the glory days of post-punk and now I was offering them something to write about. This is crucial if you are running a record label – rule one! – you must always have a good story. Writers need something to write about, and I was giving them the stories, and now I had the music to back them up. Nobody took me that seriously until I got The Jesus And Mary Chain. Then they were like, fuck, he's actually got one, and then it all blew up. Up to then, they thought I was a lovable fool, but now they thought maybe we can make a lot of money out of him!

The first Creation singles hadn't really sold, but when 'Upside Down' took off it caught the moment and the press and late-night radio were all over it. Suddenly we were selling a thousand records a day and it was hard to keep up. We spent weeks sat around in Rough Trade, folding all the sleeves and bagging them up. It was mad. I must have folded 50,000 sleeves by myself and then sent them out. That was what running a label was like at the time. It was quite literally hands-on. The Mary Chain like to think they bagged thousands of the singles as well, but it was mainly me and Joe Foster – who was now a key part of Creation, and had also produced the Mary Chain single – who did it, along with Bobby Gillespie, Dick Green and whoever else was around.

It may sound small-time – and that's because it was – but I was aiming high. It sounds crass, but it was all about winning. There was no glory for me in being stuck in a bedsit or on the dole. I was trying to escape. And with a great soundtrack – the rock 'n' roll dream! From the early days, right through to Oasis, Primal Scream and all the other bands, it was about winning and not whining, and it was about being at number 1. It would be the same later on for bands like The Stone Roses, Happy Mondays and many others. For me, punk was about being interesting and alternative, and with a different viewpoint, but still being at number 1. Creation might have been independent, but we were never 'indie'. Even when I was hanging around Rough Trade, I always hated that indie schmindie attitude. I may have been promoting underground bands, but I was also at gigs by The Jam and loved the fact that they were number 1 in the charts. This mixture of DIY and ambition was an important part of Creation.

I don't know if I thought Creation would become successful. Initially, I thought I would do it for a year and a half until the wheels came off the wagon, but at least it would be a great year with great bands. Then it happened and I thought, fuck me, it's worked! Let's keep going. It took me four years to realise Creation was a real job. Until then I was just putting records out and getting away with it. It wasn't a career, it was a passion. And then it took off…

CHAPTER 2

···

It's all about the people

I was never a conventional record company boss. Creation was never a conventional record label. People would often say that it was a maverick label and I guess that was down to me and the way I worked. Traditional labels work in a traditional way, and we were never a traditional label. Creation was always about the people.

I would often sign the person and not the song. Ironically, that was because I was a music nut and I knew that, in pop culture, the personality can be a bigger deal than the music. If you can get both then you have dynamite. Find the genuine article and you have a chance. I grew up with people like Bowie. Game-changers. One-offs. I was always interested in these types. Creative nutters. The record label can often be the first port of call for a maverick; it can be the first to recognise something in that person, the first to embrace the raw talent and believe in them. That's a big call. It could be obvious people like Bobby or Noel or Liam, or in the early days people like Stephen Pastel or Pete Astor from The Loft or Lawrence from Felt, or later with mavericks like Kevin Shields from My Bloody Valentine – all these individuals had something. You can't create characters like these. They were all different but there was something about them and their bands. They all had a unique vision of what they wanted. It was their own pop art vision and they would never compromise it. That was something I respected and was fascinated by, even though it could lead to all sorts of problems.

It was the same with the label. In a sense, we were a character label. Put me at the front and I talk it up, whilst in the background Dick Green would send out the VAT forms and do the graft and make things happen. Every band or label needs a front person. A character. A story. Maybe it was our version of the Warhol thing at The Factory in New York. I just liked to collect interesting people and see what would happen. That's how I work.

Of course, the music was the key currency at Creation as well, but it was the people and the personalities that fascinated me. I always believed that if there was charisma in the room and on the stage, then the music could be sorted afterwards. And if the characters turned up with their own songs and own ideas of how they could sound – like Oasis did – then that was all the better. But it wasn't always a problem. Having the raw personality could be enough. I always put bands with good producers to get great records and great songs out of them. What I found was that the big characters always have something creative inside them whether they know it or not; they are like magnets – ideas come to them, and my job was to get the ideas out.

It's also great if I get on with the people I'm working with, but I wouldn't say that dictates whether or not I sign them. Of course, it helps if you are pals, but you can always find a way, even if they are difficult. What I look for is just a spark in someone. It's a talent you need in something as chaotic as music. Some people have that spark but no sense of direction, and that's where I step in. I would give them a sense of direction. I would encourage them and I would organise them and I knew how to release records and not compromise them.

A lot of people would get waylaid and wonder what they were doing in the business. Others had a vision. Especially Noel Gallagher. He just knew. I think he had done his stint as a roadie with Inspiral Carpets and watched Clint Boon not quite being a superstar and was learning as he went along. To this day he's still effectively his own manager, in the sense that he knows where he's going, and he was always like that. He was a genuine character, with lots of talent and a vision – the perfect package. From the first time I saw Noel I knew he had it, and Liam as well. Noel had an indefinable quality. You could see that he had that star thing going on. Liam was totally definable. He was always going to be a star.

Oasis seemed perfect from the start. Too perfect. After I met them I kept looking for the catch but there wasn't one. It was the real thing. I kept thinking, 'Today is when I find out that they are axe murderers!', or that we would find out the real truth and it wouldn't work, but that never happened. They were actually that good. If the band hadn't happened Noel could have been the super roadie on the Manchester scene, but he ended up being the biggest star of them all. I could see that even then and it's one of the reasons I signed him. I just knew the music would come. I thought, I've caught a fucking great fucking fish, I've managed to land an amazing catch to my record label even though no one else in the music biz got it at the time. Yet we realised we had something right from the very beginning. Me and Noel sparked straight away. We were both instinctive people. From the start, both parties knew this was going to work.

Sometimes the characters I was struck by were not so obvious. Kevin Shields from My Bloody Valentine had something but I was not sure what. It was intriguing. Obviously, he's a genius, and the music he made for us was amazing, but he himself had something indefinable when I first met him. He and the band had been around us for a couple of years before we signed him to the label. It was Joe Foster who found the Valentines and brought me to see them play at a venue in Notting Hill called Bay 63 in 1986. At the time they had a singer called Dave Conway before he left to become an author, and the first thing I noticed was that drummer Colm Ó Cíosóig was a complete Keith Moon, with that wild freeform energy that drove The Who in the sixties. By 1987 My Bloody Valentine were different. They were still in that sort of vibe of their second single, 'Sunny Sundae Smile', and had a sound that was similar to Dinosaur Jr. It wasn't quite there but it was all right and I was intrigued. Then I saw them play another gig at Great Portland Street shortly afterwards, when Debbie Googe and Bilinda Butcher had joined. They sounded different and were doing a more C86 jangly indie thing, and just weren't as good as the first time I saw them. I would have given up on them there and then but they basically targeted us because Kevin loved the Mary Chain and wanted to have some kind of connection with them and Creation. So they would message us a bit but we were not initially that interested in them. Their persistence must have sparked something within me, though, because they were still on my radar.

In 1988 Biff Bang Pow! played a gig with them in Kent. We insisted on headlining as they were still unknown at the time, and the last time I'd seen them they were, as I said, like an anorak band. Big mistake. They had totally changed and were now like a psychedelic Motörhead. They blew us off the stage. It was a different thing entirely, and Kevin was now in charge of a machine. I heard his guitar and thought, what the fuck is that?, because it was so powerful. So we put them in the studio and they made this five-track EP with 'You Made Me Realise' on it. I was blown away by that song from the first time I heard it, but Kevin was not bothered by it at first. He saw it as a pastiche of Sonic Youth, but I said that's the fucking single! It's total genius!

I was close to Kevin at first and we would hang out a lot from then on in 1988. I had just broken up with my first wife, Yvonne, and Kevin and I would go to a lot of parties. We would talk about life and music, and they were good times as I got over my post-marriage problems. To this day Kevin remains an enigma but a musical genius. Probably my favourite Creation album is Primal Scream's *Screamadelica*, but My Bloody Valentine's *Loveless* is the musical masterpiece. I rarely listen to it, but in many ways it's the best record I ever put out just in terms of sound and innovation. Me and

Kevin had our fall-out but we're good with each other these days. In many ways we are quite alike – we have our vision and we are totally single-minded. That's why we eventually clashed, but then all these characters that I loved were like that – single-minded, for better or for worse.

Sometimes star quality and character are not so obvious initially but can suddenly arrive. Bobby Gillespie was already my mate from back in Glasgow, and he became a big star in the end, but at first I never saw it. He may have been my mate, and we had the bedroom band going, but there was no sign that he was ever going to be taken seriously. He was in a band called The Wake from 1981 to 1983, who were on Factory Records, but it all moved to another level when he joined The Jesus And Mary Chain and grew a fringe and became a sexy boy. We were all shocked. Overnight, he became a sex symbol on the indie scene by joining a buzz band and growing that fringe. When he didn't have the fringe he looked like the rest of us – sort of odd. And no one looked odder than me – an awkward ginger guy.

Now Bob was a sex symbol and girls tried to get to know us lot just to get to know him. Until he was twenty-one I'd never seen him with a girl, until he met this woman called Karen Parker who would go on to sing on The Jesus And Mary Chain's 'Just Like Honey' a couple of years later. Maybe he was just really shy, but we were not and when we were out we would look at girls and we would say 'she's good-looking' and he would not say a thing. He was my best friend and I never once saw him look at a girl and say he thought she was good-looking. Then he became an indie sex symbol and everything changed. Then I could see he was a star, and he was my mate, so of course I had to try and make something happen with his band. It was one of the things about running a record label – realising your mate's vision as well and making it work. It took adding Andy Weatherall to the mix in 1990 before it started working, but then Bobby was the total star. It took time but it felt inevitable.

I was really interested in all these different characters. Some of them became stars, whilst others didn't quite make it but were just as interesting. I saw something in all of them.

They each had their own unique vision; the sort of vision that we tried to realise as part of running a record label. There were people like Jerry Thackray, who became The Legend, Lawrence from Felt, Joe Foster and John Robb – all of them had a bit of rock star about them. Some never made it at all. Ed Ball was a superstar; sometimes I think that guy was a bigger star than any of them. He had played in Television Personalities and his own band, The Times, and was such a unique person, but he was never famous, though he was an amazing, larger-than-life character. I used to employ him to meet people in the

Creation office but he should have been a star. Sometimes it just doesn't happen. Of course, there was Dan Treacy as well, who had so inspired me; I should have signed him but Dan was always doing his own thing.

It might sound mad, but unless you were really interesting you could not be on the label. These days it's less important to have these characters – I mean, who knows who the guitar player in the Arctic Monkeys is, and I'm saying that as a fan. Bands now are pretty anonymous. The people on our label were all characters. Apart from maybe Teenage Fanclub, who were odd in that there was not an outrageous character in the band, but they got away with it because they could write genius songs.

In many ways, management, which is what I mainly do these days, is the same – it's all about the characters. They have to be captivating or interesting or as mad as me. All the people I manage these days are characters – Shaun Ryder, John Power from Cast, Kyle Falconer from The View, Steve Cradock from Ocean Colour Scene and the iconic Paul Cook from the Sex Pistols. They're the kind of people I'm drawn to.

The truth is that I've never done this for the money. When it came it was fantastic of course, and I looked after it, but the bottom line for me was always working with people that fascinated me. I never signed a band for the money. There were other motivations.

I remember when The Libertines fell apart and I had to choose which one to work with. They were both the sort of characters that I was drawn to. Mad, bad and dangerous to know, but full of music. Which way would I go? It was so obvious that Pete Doherty was the money shot and the best-known character, but I loved Carl Barât as a mate. Carl had been through the whole Libertines thing, when he and Pete were at each other's throats all the time and it inevitably came to an end. Carl was so good to me at that time, despite everything, and he had a new band, Dirty Pretty Things. If I was ruthless I would have gone with Doherty as he had all the big songs, but I had to go with my heart and decided to manage Carl. That's the way I've always worked. I don't always go for the money shot. I just have to be fascinated by the person – I don't even have to particularly get on with them, but Carl was a pal and a character in his own right.

Even getting off to a bad start doesn't colour my opinion of people. That danger is part of what makes them. A good example of this was Nikki Sudden and David Kusworth, who were living the rock 'n' roll dream. Nikki Sudden had been in Swell Maps, one of the great post-punk bands, and he was from the Midlands where he met David Kusworth. They both used to dress in full-on Keith Richards style and had the sound to match. They were pure rock 'n' roll and more Keef than Keef himself.

Recently I've been listening to their records. I put most of them out and it wasn't always a smooth ride. They made these great romantic rock 'n' roll records. I already loved Nikki from his days in Swell Maps. Maybe David Kusworth was the more talented of the two but Nikki was one of those nihilist types that just didn't understand the business, and maybe that's why they didn't make it, even when, as the Jacobites, they were making great records. Kusworth liked a drink and it made him more than a handful. The first time I met him he tried to punch me, even though I was releasing his album. That was not a great start to our working relationship. Sometimes I might deserve a punch, but I didn't know this guy, had never met him before, and I was putting his record out. Of course, I didn't stand back. When you are a young man from Glasgow, if you get hit then you hit back, and I floored him. Despite that, I loved his music and ended up putting out several of the albums he made with Nikki Sudden.

When you run a record label like mine and you collect these characters, they are by nature volatile and dangerous, and whether it's a punch-up or it's costing me thousands to make their album, it comes with the territory and I wouldn't have it any other way. It's what made Creation a unique label.

It was important to me to work with people who were true believers and as mad about music as I was. And this didn't just apply to the artists, but also the people that worked at Creation. I knew Dick Green because he had played the guitar with me in bands, whilst Joe Foster was my pal because I was this Television Personalities fanboy and he had played with them.

At the start of Creation, Joe was the good taste part of the label, as well as being the producer. Sometimes what he did in the studio when he worked with bands like the Mary Chain, Primal Scream, The Jasmine Minks, the Valentines and many others was really brilliant and he made the bands sound great; on other records I don't know what he did as they sounded just like a band playing in a room, which could well have been the intention. Joe definitely brought a much-needed elitism into what we did and who we signed, which was crucial. We needed a tastemaker. Back in the day that was the key. There was a snobby element in indie in those days and he sort of brought that to us. Except we were snobby about different things to everybody else. We were snobby about the Velvets, who Joe had turned me onto before anyone else was really that bothered by them – we thought they were the coolest shit.

I always worked with a tight and loyal team around me. I liked to work with people I knew. Maybe it was the Creation ideal but it was about taking your pals with you on the trip. I was into turning friends into superstars or company directors.

It was ad hoc but hugely successful. And it was not as random as it looked. I knew that even though I was the driving force and the figurehead, I needed the right people around me. Creation was not only creating underground icons out of unlikely bands, it was also creating backroom juggernauts who would run the label and make Team Creation a unique force. Like signing the bands because my instinct told me they were right, it was the same with Team Creation. The people who turned up and became part of the inner circle were the right people.

CHAPTER 3

....

Create an image and sell it

A great record label is not just about the music. No great band is just about the music. No great period of pop culture has just been about the music. It's all the other stuff as well. The culture, legends, clothes, drugs and style are just as important as the middle eight – and all this comes wrapped up in the myth. Who wants the truth when you can feel that in the music? Part of the creativity is to be larger than life. The rock stars that changed my life were out there or from outer space. We liked the stories and the myths of the bands we grew up with, like the Sex Pistols, or in the sixties The Rolling Stones, and now it was our turn, but the sucker punch was that ours were based in our warped and mad reality.

A record label needs a story, too. Creation was never ever going to be boring. For me, a great label is as rock star as the bands it represents. Of course, we would play with this. It was fucking funny. We would take the piss out of ourselves. When we set up the first Creation office at 83 Clerkenwell Road in the summer of 1985, I put a sign on my desk that said 'The President of Pop'. It was not serious. I was taking the piss. Playing with the myth. I'm just a wee ginger tool from Glasgow but I created a story around me and the label. Looking back, that sign is not that funny, but at the time it was amusing for us and it also weirdly came true.

A lot of stuff we did, people never really got. It was meant to be funny. I was laughing at myself. People thought I was trying to be a pop star because I was in a little band, but all we really wanted to do was those small German tours that were happening at the time. Those tours, organised by German indie promoter Thomas Zimmerman, would be ten gigs in really cool indie venues that each held a couple of hundred people. That was the limit of our ambition. It was our Beatles in Hamburg moment without the next bit. For a mad Glasgow kid like me, it was great to just be in a band and live the life. It was the same with the label. It was a fan's label and we created a pop culture myth and then the myth actually happened. I talked it up and told people we were going to be the biggest label in the world. I convinced myself and then everyone else, and then it happened. I knew from day one that the biggest crime in rock 'n' roll is to be boring.

We soon learned to exaggerate the truth – or, as Tony Wilson used to say, 'When forced to pick between truth and legend, print the legend.' Unlike Tony, who was a thinker, we created the legend off the cuff. We literally made it up as we went along. I'd use any trick I could to rise out of indie obscurity. I knew no one else had the balls to make these kinds of claims and then make the claims come true. I remember giving an interview in *Sounds* in 1986, and I said, 'We are the most important label in the world and one day we will have the biggest band in the world.' Of course they printed it for a laugh. For them, it was more hyperbole from a Scottish maniac, but then ten years later we really did have the biggest band in the world and we were the most important label. By then I was a drug-fuelled maniac, but it was a self-fulfilling prophecy from 'The President of Pop'. I always thought that we were going to get found out but, eventually, we manifested Oasis. We brought them to life with our mad vision.

That's the key to how the label worked, really. Some of it was a bit freaky, some of it a bit wish-fulfilment. Some of it was creating our own legend, some of it was delivering that legend. When we started, it was about being gung ho with the fanzines and even the bands themselves. It was about making everything seem bigger and more exciting than it was – how this music could change the world. It *was* based on a truth because I was genuinely excited by it all. When we got bigger, the music press were hungry for these kinds of quotes and so I kept delivering them along with made-up news stories. And when we became mainstream, the tabloids and the newspapers asked for even more stories, and I would give them stuff off the top of my head. The usual rock 'n' roll stories and mad manifestos. I was the king of that kind of shit.

Pop culture is great in that it doesn't always have to be based in truth. If a story was needed I could completely make it up, but the difference was that often I would make it happen. The creativity can be in the music but it can also be in creating the myth. The papers and the media were lapping it up, and it built the label up to be a platform and springboard for the bands. We no longer have that same sort of media culture, for better or worse, and so it's all much harder now. It's probably for the better, I guess, although it's more difficult for bands and managers who are really skint to make an impression.

Back then the *NME* news page was full of our made-up stories, like The Jesus And Mary Chain nicking their new label boss Rob Dickins's wallet – stuff like that. I knew how to work it for no money and I knew how I could wind the whole thing up. We were DIY guys. We didn't have the budget or the marketing machine so we had to make it all up. The key thing was that the bands could also deliver the music. There were a lot of great bands on other labels that never got through because they didn't get the media game. They thought the music was all you needed. Whilst the music is key, it wasn't the whole story. At Creation we knew how to make it work – I had learned from the best by watching people like Malcolm McLaren. He was a genius at the media game – look at what he did with the Sex Pistols and then with Bow Wow Wow and then his own records. He created loads of press with his stories. Although it helped that he managed the Sex Pistols, who were one of the greatest bands ever, his stories would become the narrative. He was always two steps ahead of the game because he was so immersed in pop culture. He was a manager in the same way that Bowie was a musician – he knew how to join all these bits of the story together and then take some liberties with the truth and create this amazing new world for us all to inhabit.

Maybe it's good that sort of thing doesn't exist anymore, but it was certainly a lot more colourful and fun when it did, and it was a big help in gatecrashing someone else's party or someone else's culture and getting bands heard and making them seem more exciting. Bands like The Jesus And Mary Chain were helped massively by that kind of press. The idea that they were a dangerous band or caused riots, like at North London Poly on 15 March 1985, was pretty much created by us and it got them off the ground, got them talked about. The riots were more like handbags than full-on riots, but it was all part of the story and made them more exciting and more rock 'n' roll, and the indie scene in 1985 needed that. It must have been painful for them down the track because, although they certainly had an attitude, they were never about the riots – they were about the music. In the end it nearly took them over. Like a few months later in September 1985, at the Electric Ballroom in Camden Town, when the group played six songs for twenty minutes and then fucked off, prompting the audience to destroy their equipment and rip down a lighting rig. I think the band were fed up with it by then. We knew them as pretty gentle, quiet guys, and they were hardly the type to start a riot anywhere, but creating that image around them when they came out, combined with their brilliant music, helped to get them to a big audience. Plus those riots at the early gigs were great fun to spark off.

The public image of the label, and of me, comes from those times. People have this image of me as a crazy psychotic egomaniac, but I'm much nicer in real life. These days I don't have a loud mouth. I found that difficult to maintain as I'm not really a loud-mouth type of person, but it was useful to get the label and myself a profile, and it was make or break in getting the bands noticed and heard. These days I don't have anyone doing the press or PR to blow myself up.

Running a record label is not like any other business. In other businesses, you have to be straight and you have to be together. With rock 'n' roll, sometimes the more out of it you are, the more in touch with it you are – and those wild years certainly didn't hurt the label, which was fast becoming the most successful in the UK. It's an advantage for a label to be creative with the truth or to party all weekend. It's an advantage for a label to be crazier than the bands. It's an advantage for a record label to make shit up. It's not a proper job. The madder you are, the better it gets. Until you burn out. The trouble with creating a myth is that you have to live up to that myth, and maybe that was what caused my breakdown in 1994. Of course it was a blast, but you are also immersed in the culture you are dealing with and that gets out of control.

During the time of acid house in the late eighties and early nineties, Creation was like all the myths of rock 'n' roll combined into one. We wanted to get loaded and get high. I have no idea how we released anything. I loved the whole drugs and bust-ups side of it, but I also loved the music. Much of the mythology was also the truth and the two would often get blurred. Maybe the drugs were part of what caused this blur but they were also part and parcel of the label. Nearly everyone who worked at Creation was off their heads, apart from poor old Dick Green, who ran the label while we all went crazy! Whilst we were going berserk, Dick was running the shop. We were not just printing the legend, we were living it. And snorting it. When people say never let the truth get in the way of a good story, they have no idea that in our case the truth was far more of a good story than any myth. We lived the rock 'n' roll dream and made the rest up. The trouble was that I was on a one-way track to rehab. I was living fast in the fast lane and the wheels were coming off. But I loved every minute of it.

The other part of Creation's image was the artwork. Creation itself was steeped in pop art. Everything always looked great. Pop art fucked with the narrative and created ideas and changed the way you thought about the role of music and the world. My real interest in it came from being into sixties bands like The Creation, then finding out about Andy Warhol and The Velvet Underground, and then the wider circle of people like David Hockney and in more recent times Howard Hodgkin. As a teenager, I loved Warhol and other pop art but I'm not sure I understood it, I just loved looking at it, which is maybe all you need. You can just feel it. Like the music.

Whilst maybe I didn't understand the Velvets and Warhol at first, I knew they were cool, and my Communication Blur fanzine was heavily influenced by artworks like Roy Lichtenstein's 'Whaam!', or by Dan Treacy. I had these really in-depth conversations with Dan about pop art and how it turned art and culture upside down and was a revolt in style against the traditional views of what art should be. Suddenly art was no longer stuffy museum pieces or contained in galleries. A new generation of artists made art out of the everyday. Their own lives were the template, their own reality the canvas. Punk was built from these fundamentals and at Creation we turned it into a lifestyle.

Pop art played a part in the artwork – and economics – of the early Creation releases. I knew what I was doing when I was ripping off the Fire Engines' 'Candyskin' plastic bag packaging for those early Creation singles. Me, Gillespie and Innes were obsessed with the Fire Engines, their sound and aesthetic. Also, the sleeves cost eighty quid rather than six hundred and they looked better as well.

The pop art influence was more than just record sleeves, though. We knew that creating an image was important if we were going to be successful. We were into this cool mod style, mixed with the Television Personalities and influenced by The Byrds and the Velvets.

Despite loving the music and art, ultimately, looking back, I think I'm talentless, but I can make things happen. Maybe that's the talent. I created the legend and then made it happen.

CHAPTER 4

....

Entering the big time

The success of The Jesus And Mary Chain changed things, launching Creation into the big league – or the bigger indie league. It put the spotlight on the label and we were now centre stage. I was managing the band as well and the money they made was keeping the label afloat. They moved on after their first single, but it meant that the attention was now on us. It was our first taste of the real music biz beyond the DIY world, and all eyes were watching our next move. We were hoping for another band to take off in the same kind of way but, looking back, we were still very much an underground label. It was a confusing period. The success saw Warners offer me my own label in 1986, to run as well as Creation, which we called Elevation Records. It was my first taste of the world of majors but, despite having a good stable of bands like The Weather Prophets (who had emerged from the ashes of The Loft), Primal Scream and Edwyn Collins, we didn't get the instant hits they were expecting and the label folded.

Still, after the Mary Chain success, Creation now had more clout and we could sign bigger bands. Being able to sign Felt to the label in 1986 felt like a big deal to me. I'd been friends with the band's singer, Lawrence, since 1984. I'd met him in the early days when I was looking for bands to create some kind of scene and was being drawn to these maverick characters who seemed to thrive in the most unlikely places. Lawrence was living in Birmingham and I met him when I was twenty-three and he was slightly younger, maybe twenty-one. In my world, Lawrence was a big star, already an indie icon in a very small scene. In 1985 Lawrence and Felt left Cherry Red Records and I heard on the grapevine that they wanted to be on Creation. We couldn't believe it. At the time, Cherry Red was one of the big indie labels who had signed bands like Dead Kennedys, The Monochrome Set and Everything But The Girl. In many ways we aspired to be a label like Cherry Red – even more than Rough Trade. They seemed to have the perfect setup and way of doing things. They signed really cool bands and made it work. They had an aesthetic and were organised. They were smart and successful and had great ideas.

Felt's music was steeped in indie cool and photogenic surliness, and they seemed bolted on for the big time but ended up being too good. It's weird to think now, but at the time I felt out of my depth signing them. It was the equivalent of me being this little ginger dude and getting a really good-looking woman to go out with me! We still saw ourselves as just a bedroom label and they'd had been on an actual proper record company, but it made perfect sense aesthetically. We had the same reference points and a love of the same culture.

The music press were all over us now, our operation was building and the label had a growing underground following. We were becoming notorious and that was a good thing. The Mary Chain riots had made the label look and feel dangerous and we certainly had an attitude, which is important when you are finding your way as a label – it was a combination of what I felt inside and also of how we needed to get heard through all the noise. I was in my Malcolm McLaren period, and dressed like him in all his 1977 Sex Pistols glory, with my leathers and the same curly ginger hair, and I was also in the same combative mode. I would tell people to fuck off, or make outrageous statements, like telling journalists that 'This is truly art as terrorism' after a riot that I had partly caused at The Jesus and Mary Chain gig. Everybody at Creation was playing a role. It was part of the story. We were walking and talking the myth. We were into the drama of it all. The music business is a ridiculous occupation and I was a ridiculous human being, but it was perfect and just added to the story.

By 1985 we were more than a bedroom label. We had our office in Farringdon and were in the mix as one of the upcoming indie labels but, until The House of Love came along in 1987, we were still no closer to breaking out like we had done with the Mary Chain single, though you could feel it coming. The mid-eighties were like our indie years, and that was not what I was interested in. Aesthetically it was good – that was the big thing. The music was on our own terms and we were releasing good stuff like Joe Foster's band Slaughter Joe and also Meat Whiplash, The Bodines, The Moodists and even Bill Drummond – the maverick's maverick, who would go on to put KLF together not too long after. All great stuff but we wanted to take that music, and that ideal of the pop art punk explosion, into the mainstream. It was only a matter of time.

Although breaking the Mary Chain meant that we were seen as a serious label for a bit, the music papers, who were the arbiters of cool at that time, suddenly decided we were now somehow uncool. They decided that music had changed and we were getting left behind and needed to sign and break a band as big as the Mary Chain. It was really difficult for us in 1987, with finances and direction, and we lurched from one crisis to another. We needed to find a band to change the narrative and get us back on track. Like all labels sometimes, we needed a change of direction. We had a few bands that could have done it but for one reason or another they just didn't break through. Part of being an indie label is to be on the edge and part of it is to somehow survive. We needed the band that was of the moment, the game-changer. And that's when The House of Love arrived.

The House of Love was an amazing band and the next major part of the label's story. They became the bridge between the tail end of the Mary Chain era and the soon-to-come boom time Creation of My Bloody Valentine, Slowdive and Ride. I took a massive gamble with them and they broke big and then all hell broke loose. They made brilliant records but were quite a handful to deal with. Even for us. At their peak, though, I loved them and they could have taken on anybody live. Guy Chadwick was a master songwriter and Terry Bickers was a true genius on the guitar – it was a perfect combination. They had the recipe for success and the album was huge, and it saved the label at a point when we had hit a financial rock bottom because our recent signings had not taken off. With the success, though, came the craziness. It always goes bonkers when a band takes off, and for a time they were *the* band.

I first came across The House of Love in 1986 when I met Guy Chadwick, who was a massive Mary Chain fan and had left a demo of his song, 'Shine On', at the office. I did have a listen to it but it didn't really grab me at first. Initially, I thought that it was too Mary Chain sounding, and also too pop and too pretty, so I passed on it. Then someone in the office, I think it was Dick, started playing the demo over and over again and I heard it blasting out of the speakers and I said, that's fucking great – let's put it out! Maybe this was a case of delayed instinct... So we went to see them support The Primitives in London at the back end of 1986 and it was pretty good but it needed more focus. All the songs were seven minutes long, so I spoke to them after the gig and said, you're a great band, but let's change the hippy jam band thing and make the songs three minutes long and cut all the crap and the jamming out.

By the time they supported my band Biff Bang Pow! at the Black Horse in Camden in early 1987 they had the thing down and the songs were much punchier. We then signed them and I started managing them as well, but when we put out the first single, 'Shine On', only a few people liked it, like the music journalist Danny Kelly. Then we released 'Real Animal' as the second single and that didn't really happen either, apart from a bit of play on Janice Long on nighttime BBC radio. At this point, I was deeply committed to the band. I had no choice but to carry on as I was gambling everything on them. Yvonne and I were splitting up and she got my house and my pension when we got divorced. I was down on my luck. Not only had Yvonne cleaned me out but the Mary Chain had sacked me as manager in 1986 because they wanted to be taken seriously as a musical force and not for the riots. They wanted a professional setup and we were too amateur at the time. Recent releases hadn't sold as much as we'd hoped and I was even thinking that maybe I'd have to become a labourer after all. But I believed in The House of Love so much that I staked everything I had on them. Running an indie label is always a gamble, though, and I had nothing to lose. Literally. So I took all the money I had left in the world and put it into the band. I banked it all on The House of Love.

The album was being produced by Pat Collier, who was mixing it with Guy. I went down to the studio to have a listen. It sounded like an art album, with the vocals mixed down too low and submerged in the noise. I said the vocals have to sit on top and I told Pat Collier this is how I want it to be, so I spent my last twelve grand in the world on getting the album mixed properly. This is the kind of brinkmanship you have to be prepared for when you run an indie record label. I gambled the last of my money, and to my absolute amazement their next single, 'Christine', exploded – mainly because it's a great song and a brilliant performance that really caught the moment. Then the album followed and sold 500,000 copies worldwide, and Creation was back in business financially, but also with a genius album which was even more important.

Acid house had not yet happened by 1987/88 and everything still revolved around bands. The press was going crazy for The House of Love, so I put them out on a seventy-date tour in ninety days, in places like Leamington Spa, and that kinda made their album even bigger when it came out in 1988 and took it into the top ten. I then acted as their manager and signed The House of Love to a major called Fontana for a fortune, because classic guitar bands were still where it was at for big labels.

Guy Chadwick was a real talent and The House of Love were one of my favourite bands – and that's not just because I was their manager. They were genius and Guy was a great songwriter, but he was also an absolute nihilist who fucks things up because that's the way he is. I respect that. That's the punk part of my thinking. The big crossroads came when Terry Bickers left the band – or Guy sacked him (they both claim different things) – just before the second album came out. There were a lot of mad people in that band, but Terry was probably the maddest and the music press was full of his escapades and spaced-out quotes every week. But if it was a case of Guy throwing Terry out, then that was such an own goal because, as good as Guy was, Terry was an incredible guitar player and maybe the real star of the band. Guy had tried to throw him out a few times before and I'd stopped him from doing it, but this time I was in LA when he finally went. Like I said, Guy was nihilistic like a lot of creative people, but I think I got the best out of him.

The band was breaking pretty big in 1988 and into 1989, and then, overnight, the scene went Madchester and acid house and it was not about indie anymore and the band were in danger of being marooned by fashion. Acid house turned everything upside down. Guy would turn up at the all-night parties we were having at Creation and would do some really crazy stuff – crazier than anyone else, and we were all pretty crazy. The band were still doing well but Guy had his own vision and I pulled back a bit from managing them. Eventually, he phoned me up and said, I'm sacking you. I remember putting the phone down and saying, 'Yes!' I was so relieved. I wanted out. For me, once Terry was no longer in the band it was a different group and had become more of a solo project for Guy. I think Guy wrote a lot of those lead guitar lines but no one could play them like Terry Bickers – he was a real guitar hero and together they were a brilliant team.

Despite all we went through, I'm still friends with Guy. He asked me to do a recent American tour, and if he asked me to manage The House of Love again, I would still do it as I genuinely love the band. They were a great Creation band. The songs stand up and they were brilliantly written and balanced out the band's madness. For one year they could have taken anyone on live. I loved them and was gutted they never stayed at Creation and went to the majors.

CHAPTER 5

·····································

Stay loyal to
your artists and friends

My life has been a tale of two cities. I've lived in London for years, but I've never lost my Scottish core. These days I am a product of both Glasgow and London, and Creation – whilst being very much a London operation – always had that twist of Glasgow at its heart, with a circle of Scottish pals making up much of the music and the label's identity. A lot of people remained in the Creation orbit for decades. I may have been into these mad characters and mavericks, but it was never a flavour of the month thing for me. I was always loyal to people. I think that's important in something like the music business, which is notoriously fickle.

Bobby Gillespie is a central character in the Creation story and was key to the vision, but working together sometimes damaged our friendship. He might not see it, but I think it did. We were good friends before punk, and after it changed our lives we were even bigger pals. Over the years we've had our ups and downs like all friends. He's a very difficult person, but then I'm a very difficult person as well. Probably even more so. Don't get me wrong – I love Bobby, but working with each other has had its issues. Saying that, he has been crucial to the label, and his guidance has been vital at many points. He brought some of the bands in to the label and tipped me off about others. It started with The Jesus And Mary Chain because he'd heard them when he was in Glasgow running his Splash One club. At the time they were called the Daisy Chain and had sent a cassette of early versions of 'Never Understand' and 'Upside Down' to a promoter at the Candy Club in Glasgow, trying to get a gig. They were turned down, but the promoter passed the tape on to Bobby Gillespie because it had a compilation of Syd Barrett stuff on the other side, and when he flipped the tape over from the Syd stuff he heard the two demos. He thought they were great and sent the tape on to me. That's how it worked. It was our own musical daisy chain. A label is lucky to have someone like that. Someone who gets it. Someone who knows the idea behind it all.

Bobby himself had been busy since The Drains. He was in the Glasgow band The Wake in the early 1980s, and was also deeply involved with the mid-1980s Splash One club nights that played host to bands like Sonic Youth, BMX Bandits, Wire, The Pastels, The Loft, Submarines, The Jasmine Minks and The Shop Assistants, and then he was the stand-up drummer oozing indie cool in The Jesus And Mary Chain. Then he put together Primal Scream – the archetypal Creation band, who navigated the choppy waters of the indie scene before emerging in full bloom in acid house with perhaps the greatest synthesis of indie dance music. The ultimate fans' band, Primal Scream was a group born out of record collections, late-night conversations on rock 'n' roll and dreaming up music from the scrapbooks of golden pop moments. They would become the band who were in some ways the heart and soul of Creation. Maybe Bobby believed in Creation even more than I did. He certainly understood the aesthetic inside out.

He was always trying to help everyone out. It was very altruistic of him. He would phone me up and say, 'McGee, you've got to put this band out...' and me being me would sign them. Teenage Fanclub were a perfect example. They were headlining at Koko in London and had already released a mini album, *A Catholic Education*, in 1990 on Paperhouse

Records; they were kinda big in a cult indie way. I was aware of them but Bobby framed it for me and raved about them and their songwriting and their melodies, and when I went to see them I totally got it, and the band wanted to move to Creation. Sometimes it makes sense for a band to change label. Creation was a bigger label than they were on and we could get them to where they needed to be. Plus they are a Glasgow band and we spoke the same language with the same accent, which probably confused the fuck out the English. All these Scottish bands, like Scottish people generally, just don't trust the English or Londoners, so I was, like, their representative in the city; I spoke just like them and so they were prepared to talk to me and not the English idiot guy who talked down to them just because they were Scottish. The bands said, hang on, let's go with McGee because he is one of us. And I was. It also helped that I had been in bands as well. I knew the language musically and geographically.

Another example of Bobby tipping me off on stuff was when he came into the office in 1997 and said that I had to re-sign The Jesus And Mary Chain. It had been years since he had drummed for them or I had managed them. It had been a long jaunt for all of us since we were first involved in 1984. At that time the band had become the coolest group in the UK and went on to a major label and have proper hits before Bobby had left to do the Primals. They then dumped me as manager, which upset me at the time, but I don't blame them. It was all crazy then. After that, even if it had been diminishing returns for them after those early years when they were the hottest band in the country, they still sold a lot of records. By the mid-nineties, though, they had fallen out of favour. Music had moved on and acid house had changed things. The scene had changed and the bands had changed. Rock 'n' roll had changed. Even Primal Scream had got out of their leathers. The Jesus And Mary Chain were still a good band but were just out of favour. It happens. It's what you know when you run a record label. There is an upside and then a downside. Things move on and you have to be aware. How do you keep your vision current without compromising it? It's a test for anyone involved in music.

Anyway, by 1997, no one else would put their album out. After Bobby spoke to me, I got their new demos sent over and they sounded great – not classic Mary Chain but they were still pretty good. Maybe it was sentimental and maybe I should have followed one of the best pieces of advice you get from football – that when a manager goes back to an old club to revive the glory days, it never works out, but maybe I wanted to get in touch with those early days of Creation and the Mary Chain again. That rush of energy I'd had before the burnout had been an exciting and special time for us all. The Mary Chain was a reminder of the frisson and excitement of the old days of the label from a time when it felt punk rock and dangerous. Of course, in pop culture you know that things move and change and things can never be the same again, but it doesn't stop you chasing it.

I offered them a sixty-grand advance, which was pretty generous considering where they were at that point in time in the market. Then, on the day of the signing, they asked for the cost of recording on top of that. That was cheeky. Normally we would have shown a band the door at that point. No one else in the music biz was interested in them so we held all the cards. I could have shown them the door and they would have had no option, but maybe because of the old days or maybe because now I could actually get the money, we gave them the deal.

That's when running a maverick label works against you. We were not running a normal record company, making decisions based solely on good business. I was still doing deals on a whim and sometimes with a sentimental twist, and I was loyal to people like Bobby and the Mary Chain. That was part and parcel of Creation. The Mary Chain had been so important to our story, and all our lives had changed when we met. It needed to be done. We released their *Munki* album in 1998 and it did ok and got into the bottom end of the top 50, and a year later they split up. It would be a few more years before we would work together again, when I was brought back as manager for a short time to get the band back on course after they had drifted again.

Primal Scream were always my main band, though. They were the core of Creation. It was that friendship thing, plus I knew they had something special about them. They were not always the biggest band on the label, though, and it must have been hard for Bobby when Oasis took off, but he never bitched about it. Me and Bobby had been there since the beginning. Early on, I knew Bobby was getting a band together – they supported The Laughing Apple when we went back to play in Glasgow in the early eighties – and I was always going to work with him. In 1985 I released their debut single, 'All Fall Down', because they were not only writing brilliant songs but we both understood what this was all about.

Before Oasis, Creation had been all about Primal Scream, and then suddenly the label was all about Oasis. Oasis were not only the biggest band in the culture and in the country, they were actually on my record label. That's a hard pill for the other bands on the label to swallow. Oasis were so big that they completely overshadowed the label, yet Primal Scream just got on with business. Bobby probably saw it as being good for the cause, because he believed in what the label was about. Oasis were twenty times bigger than everybody else put together, but not twenty times better, and we had to be twenty times more involved. Success on that scale is ironically hard to handle for a record label. Coping with the sheer scale of it and still trying to find time for all the other bands was a real challenge. The upside is that it reflects back on the label and the other bands, but trying to keep everyone involved at the same kind of level is not easy. It was a real balancing act.

I don't think anybody's made a better album than Primal Scream's *Screamadelica*. It was always my favourite on Creation, which might be because it's musically brilliant, and because I love Bobby and Andrew Innes and we go all the way back to our bedroom band, but it's also because of the vision. These were my boys, and it made me feel so proud that they had pulled this off. I have known them both for such a long time. Andrew's involvement with the label and the band has been key as well, but people do not really know Andrew because he just doesn't talk to anybody. When was the last time he did an interview? 1983?

You have to remember that band were my close pals, so it was truly tragic when their guitar player Robert Young – or 'Throb' as he was nicknamed – died in 2014. Not only was he a great guitar player but he was a pal from back at school in Glasgow. He was part of the inner circle. Throb was strong, whilst the rest of us were weak, and we all fucking collapsed because of the drugs and the craziness and had to get clean, but with Throb being the horse that he was, he just kept going. There's a lot of death around Primal Scream, if you think about it. The price can be high and it was tragic to lose not only Throb but also their singer Denise Johnson, producer Andy Weatherall, and Paul Cannell, who designed the band's iconic logo, over the years.

Primal Scream were the real deal in that they lived rock 'n' roll 24/7. It's amazing that none of us ever got arrested. When I went to rehab, the Primals didn't blink, and just carried on with the mad party that involved most of them. I don't think they could get their heads around where I was at then. When I left rehab they just didn't understand the changes I had to make. They didn't get that I had to leave drugs and parties behind. Shortly after rehab, I went to see them play in Liverpool, and the surrounding drugs and craziness were too much for me in the fragile state I was in at the time. I was not in that world anymore and I decided then that I needed a break from the band. I knew our friendship wouldn't survive if I was drawn back into that mad chemical band world that had nearly destroyed me, so I had to take time out from that world and Bobby and the band. Those friendships ran deep and went back to our Glasgow days. It was a reminder that there were bonds far deeper and more important than the label itself.

Saying that, I was still there for them when I was needed. Bobby would ring up now and then for advice or the other way round, and we would talk about music and his career. There was the time in 1997 when the band were coming back with new stuff and a new album, *Vanishing Point*. The album was pretty dark and off the wall, bonkers and total genius. I loved it. The rest of Creation wasn't so sure, and they didn't want to release 'Kowalski' as the lead single. By then, the people that worked at Creation were not the same mad crew that started the label. They knew how to work in the music business but they didn't quite get Creation. It was a rock 'n' roll label, not a corporate machine. Of course we wanted success, but it had to be on our terms. That's how mad we were. After *Screamadelica* and then its follow-up *Give Out But Don't Give Up*, the label had expected the band to stay fairly commercial, but 'Kowalski' was too left-field and they were panicking. From my semi-retirement, I put my foot down and insisted 'Kowalski' was the single, and then it went top 10 and the album was top 3, so me and Bobby were right. That felt good and it meant that, even if me and Bobby didn't see eye to eye all the time, the bond was deeper than that and we were on the same side in the music war trenches.

STAY LOYAL TO YOUR ARTISTS AND FRIENDS

They say that in this business you should not work too closely with your friends, but we broke that rule. It was fundamental to this story and to the label that my closest friend, who I had an on/off friendship with for years, was in the label's core band and key to this whole thing.

CHAPTER 6

....

The art of A&R

Historically, A&R – Artists and Repertoire – was the part of a record label or music publishing company that was responsible for talent scouting and overseeing the artistic development of recording artists and songwriters. By the post-punk era, it meant so many different things, from signing the bands to helping to shape their careers. It's perhaps the dark art at the heart of a record label: how do you sign and turn a band into something successful without ruining what made it so raw and magical in the first place? For many labels, this was the chance to chip all the edges away from something thrilling and make it a commodity, often ruining it in the process. For a maverick label like Creation, of course, it was always going to be a very different process.

When you sign bands, sometimes you let them get on with it and give them the freedom they need. This was the case with Stephen and his band The Pastels, and with The Membranes, where you let them make records for better or worse. But some bands can't handle that and it gets chaotic, or nothing happens. You then have to try and guide them in their musical vision, or in how to be in a band, and sort out any inter-band politics. You have to work out the fundamental stuff, like how and when to tour or how to make records. Sometimes you have to dig out genius, when you know it's there but they don't. Sometimes you have to work surreptitiously to subtly change what a band is doing for the better.

Initially, with Primal Scream I let them make what they wanted. When that wasn't working, I got involved to try and shape it into something that maybe somebody would eventually buy. And it worked. Of course, Bobby knew his pop culture as well, but he was failing badly, even if the first album was perfect guitar pop. By the second eponymous album released in 1989, the band had musically gone full leather-trousered rock 'n' roll, whilst the music scene was heading towards acid house. A full-on rock 'n' roll band – even a great one – was out of step with the times. When you are in a band, or part of something like that, you can't always see the bigger picture or know what you have got. Primal Scream had tried The Byrds for the first album and then the New York Dolls for the second album, and it just wasn't working. A key part of running a record label is to have this overview and then make something happen. Most labels would have board meetings and bring in the accountants. My method was to hit the clubs and go fucking mental.

Maybe it was partly an accident and maybe it was partly by design, but we got Bobby into ecstasy and raves, and this was the game-changer that we'd all been looking for, though not in the most obvious way. The band turned up to the clubs in their rock 'n' roll gear and met acid house halfway, and then something wonderful happened. All I was doing was saying to the Primals that there was this new scene that was fucking amazing, that they should come down to the clubs and check it out. Did I think it was going to end up with them making *Screamadelica*? Probably not. I was just sharing my enthusiasm for the biggest cultural revolution since punk, but it was the spark they needed and they were cool enough to do something of their own with it.

My initial ambition was maybe to hear a remix of a Primal Scream track getting played at a club so that I could dance to it. I know that sounds mental but I was just looking for one twelve-inch remix. I just wanted to go to a club like Shoom,

Spectrum or Land Of Oz that would have a Creation record remixed and played over the PA whilst we were off our heads on E. It would be like the perfect meeting of two worlds!

Maybe that's what A&R is about as well. It's about being there. On the cutting edge. Checking it out and connecting it with your bands and seeing what happens. Being an instigator and a troublemaker. Seeing what can be done to get bands heard without ruining them and what they are about. Being creative with ideas. In a sense, A&R is about bringing people together and sparking something quite different. I kinda engineered that by getting Andy Weatherall together with Primal Scream for the remix of 'I'm Losing More Than I'll Ever Have'. His first attempt was pretty straight, but the band told him to do it again and fucking destroy the track, which he did and came up with something that was total genius and eventually became 'Loaded', which was a game-changer and where indie and dance collided perfectly. It was a hit, and then he co-produced the *Screamadelica* album and that was the moment. From going out to these clubs, I already knew people like Andy, though he wasn't that famous a face at the time. He was part of the Boy's Own crowd, who were running around the acid house scene with their own fanzine and putting on their own parties. They had their own thing going on. In that scene, Terry Farley and Danny Rampling were much more famous than Andy at that point, but he was into The Clash and indie as well so we had a common ground.

I was a music fanatic, and that appealed to a lot of people and to many of the bands. I was as obsessed as they were. I was actually genuinely fascinated by bands and rock 'n' roll and making records. I was also living the lifestyle. Creation was like a band – in fact we were more rock 'n' roll than most of the bands! For me, you had to be steeped in the stuff. I was fascinated by pop culture and music and records – that's got to be crucial if you are running a record label, especially one like Creation. I was a cultural provocateur, though not as much as Malcolm McLaren, who was a hero to me and who changed the fabric of culture beyond music. Malcolm understood the bigger picture. That was his genius. He could tie music, art, culture and politics together. His vision was mind-blowing. I was just a wee music guy but I sold millions more records!

With acid house, we were hanging out in the clubs and having a great time. We didn't have a cultural master plan like creating a fusion between indie and dance like Malcolm would have done. It was as simple as let's add the new dance culture and sounds to some of our own records and encourage that to happen and see what comes out. Once it really started to come together like on *Screamadelica*, it was mind-blowing. There were some amazing remixes and some amazing music.

It was like my two musical worlds had come together, and it was breaking boundaries and you could dance to it when you were off your head in a club. Perfect.

I guess this was our kind of A&R in action. We were not sitting in an office plotting the future. We were out there in the middle of it. It was like a fan's A&R more than a business A&R, driven more by curiosity than dollars. Sometimes I would do the A&R, but quite often it was a team effort, with everyone throwing ideas in. It could be me, it could be the bands, it could be the people in the office, or people like Jeff Barrett, who was doing my PR at the time and now runs Heavenly Recordings. Everyone put ideas in the pot. We were a collective gang running around the acid house scene and getting into all this new stuff and it was rubbing off on everyone.

Some of the ideas worked and some didn't. We once wasted five grand on a remix that was fucking shit. It was the early days of doing remixes and Throb had an idea of who he wanted to try as a remixer, so we used him and he was totally the wrong guy for Primal Scream and we ended up with this terrible Italian house remix that definitely wasn't the vision I was after. Ultimately though, it was the collective thing that was important with Primal Scream, that pool of ideas that everyone was throwing into. I could lie and change the story to say it was me that got Bobby into acid house, but that's not what happened. The great thing about *Screamadelica* was that it was a collective mix of ideas (and drugs, probably) that made that record.

A&R was not always like this for bands on the label. There were different scenarios for dealing with different people, like Kevin from My Bloody Valentine. I don't regret making the My Bloody Valentine album, *Loveless*, no matter how much it cost me – how could you regret its genius? But the actual experience of making it certainly wasn't enjoyable, and was a financial nightmare. It was the hardest record I've ever had to get through. In 1989 we were a little label in a little office. Even with no money we spent thousands on that Valentines record – thousands that we just didn't have! With Kevin, we suggested loads of things and they were all resisted. We didn't mind because the great thing about the label – unlike major labels – was that we actually let the people be themselves. Even if it cost us.

I remember at the time going to one of the many studios that Kevin seemed to be using to see where the album was up to. We just dropped by as we hadn't heard from the band for some time and had not heard the album that we were paying a fortune for. When we got there, Kevin played me some stuff and that's when I first heard *Loveless*. I remember feeling more than a little bemused with what I heard, and I was shouting, 'I've spent a quarter of a million fucking pounds on this and I can't even hear the fucking vocals!' The album had already taken two and a half years to make and had nearly bankrupted us and nearly given me a breakdown. It even turned Dick's hair grey! I had to borrow money from my father, and from my mum's life insurance policy to complete the album. It ruined my relationship with the band but, in the end, it resulted in a stunning album that Bobby Gillespie astutely calls the last great rock record that went somewhere new.

But it was impossible working with Kevin, even though he is a genius – or maybe because he is a genius. He's a lovely person but a nightmare, because he has a vision and it takes years to get the vision to work. Fuck knows where his head was at between their debut album, *Isn't Anything,* which we released in November 1988, and *Loveless,* which was eventually released in November 1991. Maybe he was into drugs? He never looked like he was, but how could we tell? We were doing more drugs than anyone. We were so far out of it that there was no going back. We were also deep into making this album. I guess if you were running a record label properly, then this would have been the moment to rein the band in or pull the plug, but that wasn't how I ran a record label. I spent every penny I had on that record and Kevin would not even let me in the studio for months to listen to it. Maybe that's the price you have to pay for that kind of talent, and it was certainly a big price. With *Isn't Anything,* he had gone from being in what people saw as an also-ran band to being the leader of the new music scene. The record sparked what was known as the shoegazing scene and was one of the albums of the year. It was a game-changer. Kevin's music was now off the scale. It was futuristic. No one was there to plot where he was going apart from him. No wonder it ended up in a situation like this. He was so far into the future that there was no one to ask. There was no road map, and unfortunately I was bankrolling it.

Other bands could be totally different. When we signed Teenage Fanclub, they went up to Liverpool's Amazon Studios to record their album *Bandwagonesque* and we just left them to it. I was expecting a pretty good indie album, but then we went up to hear it in 1991 and every track was a classic. Of course, they were always great, but I seriously thought they would be an indie-type band and sell 50,000 tops. I didn't think they were going to be that huge because, to me, they were great songwriters but not at the fame and fortune level of some other bands. When I heard *Bandwagonesque*, though, I honestly thought, wow, that's brilliant, total genius, but to sell as many as it did was something else. Suddenly I realised that we had three big bands on the label, with Teenage Fanclub now joining Primal Scream and The Valentines. It was totally unexpected. The album sold 200,000 in Europe and the same in the States and was a major player. Ironically, we got much more involved in the follow-up, *Thirteen*, and it only sold 150,000 worldwide. The songs were still good but the sound was a bit flat. My A&R suggestion for that album had been bringing in someone like Youth to produce it, and changing things around, maybe getting a hip-hop beat in there on a track. Bands go to people like Youth with half an album and end up with their most acclaimed release. Just listen to the Verve's 'Bitter Sweet Symphony', which was carved by Youth. He really knows what he is doing, but Teenage Fanclub had their own idea and fair play to them. I respect that and was just making suggestions.

I think the success of *Bandwagonesque* actually unhinged the band a bit. Initially, they were more like an early Creation band, and not the sort of band you would have thought would get a sniff of the mainstream. After *Bandwagonesque* you would get labels like Geffen saying to them, 'You could be the new Nirvana,' and that really freaked them out. It would freak anyone out at that point in time. To be honest, it freaked Nirvana out to be Nirvana.

In other cases, we would be a bit more hands-on with a band's A&R. If things were not working with a band we would sometimes step in and make a big decision, like when I scrapped the first Oasis album because the production wasn't right. Initially produced by Dave Batchelor, who Noel knew from his days working as a roadie for Inspiral Carpets, and then mixed by Mark Coyle, it just didn't have the big sound they had live. It was recorded twice and mixed three times at a cost of £50,000 – a huge gamble but I knew there was something more in the sound and we had to get it. It was the same when I scrapped Primal Scream's follow-up to *Screamadelica*, *Give Out But Don't Give Up*, because the production by Tom Dowd wasn't working. Primal Scream had got their Les Pauls out again, but I thought those Memphis sessions were too flat. It was just not right for them. We then got George Drakoulias in to do it and it sounded much better. With those two albums, these were key decisions and someone had to make them. That's the art of A&R. The crucial tweak or decision. Just getting in there and fucking fixing it. Decisions like that change not just an album but the course of a band's career. If I had allowed the original Dave Batchelor version of the Oasis record to be released, we would not be living in Oasis culture now. They went through a few producers to try and get it right. When they brought in Owen Morris, I was dubious at first. At that point he was Johnny Marr's engineer, who had worked with Electronic, so he had a bit of a track record but not enough, I thought, for what was needed. But the wall of sound he brought to the tracks by turning everything up to full sounded bang on and was perfect for the band. If that had not been done then Oasis would have been a one-album band.

In general, though, I didn't get over-involved with the bands. My way of working has always been more like, there's the studio, there's the keys, now get on with it and make the fucking record. I think a lot of our success as a label was because we allowed bands space to breathe, with just an occasional nudge. The really great stuff like *Screamadelica*, *Loveless*, *Bandwagonesque* and *Definitely Maybe* came from letting the bands get on with it, and it totally fucking works because the people making those records are actually on a total fucking roll and it just gets bigger and bigger. All you have to do is let them be themselves and it explodes. Letting them be is an A&R skill. If it ain't broke, don't fix it.

On the other hand, there's a whole raft of bands that we probably should have got more involved with, and that didn't always happen. Bands don't ask for help, but maybe we should have stepped in and got more involved anyway. Whether it's musical advice or general life advice, a bit of A&R can be a game-changer. Adorable were an indie band from Coventry that we signed in 1992, and we should have given them more guidance. When we first signed them, they came down to the office. They were a great band but they just got off on the wrong foot. The Creation office, at that point, was run by people like Bobby Gillespie's ex-girlfriend and Jim Reid's partner, Laurence Verfaillie, who worked there doing press. We looked after people and gave all my friends' girlfriends jobs because they were our pals and they were also good at what they did. They were all cool women and key to the label. Adorable said some stuff on that first trip, the sort of stuff that bands would say in those days – about Jim Reid being too old, or about Bobby not making it – to the whole office, not just to their partners. Yet the whole office loved Jim and Bobby and they hated Adorable for that. Creation was really tight-knit. It was like an extended family and Adorable lost the dressing room. They were a good band and they should have made it and I should have had a word with them before all that happened. That's another part of good A&R – it's not only about the music but sometimes about how to play the game.

Managing bands is a very different role from running a label, and I will step in more. I got involved with The Libertines for their second album and they were the hardest band I have ever worked with, completely out of control. And I had worked with some pretty out-of-control people, myself included. The band members were in different places and Peter was quite smacked out and also pissed off with Carl at this point. My personal take on it is that he didn't want to give Carl the songs he was working on at the time for the album. These were songs like 'Can't Stand Me Now', 'Music When The Lights Go Out', 'The Man Who Would Be King', 'Hooligans On E' and 'What Katie Did', which he may have wanted for his new Babyshambles project. When the album was being recorded, Peter barely came down for the sessions. He was there maybe eight times in two months to do bits and would then fuck off. Luckily, for some reason he would listen to me. So I had a sort of plan, which was to let him do his heroin and then for a twenty-minute window afterwards when he was pliable, I would be in the studio and encourage him to do two takes of each song in that short window of time. So we got good versions of all the songs with the band, except for 'Hooligans On E', which he had written with Pete Welsh from the band Kill City in Cardiff's Marriott Hotel whilst both their bands were touring. We never got that one down properly. Both their bands demoed it and there is a Libertines version but it never got finished.

And that's A&R in action. You have to deal with really fucking odd situations and try to make them work. The results tell the story. Did the Libertines album go to number 1 and sell a million records? Yes, it did. The previous record sold 30,000 records and got to number 35, so this album was the big one. We did really well. I managed to squeeze the songs out of Peter and add them to the other great songs on the album and make a classic that they can live and tour off forever if they want to. But at what cost? The band was broken after that but, as their live agent Russell Warby said to me, it was already being held together with Elastoplast anyway.

Ultimately, A&R is an instinctive balancing act. You do it on a case-by-case basis and it can be different for every band. It's down to what feels right. The art is to seize the day. It's about finding solutions to problems. It's about getting the wheels back on and it's about doing whatever it takes as you steer the ship to shore.

CHAPTER 7

....

Go where the action is

I'm lucky to be the age I am. I lived through the main music revolutions: punk rock and acid house – the two musical movements that changed everything. And I was on the barricades both times. Pogoing and raving. I was a teenager for punk rock and bought all the records, and ten years later I was twenty-seven and still just young enough to get into acid house. I was also running a label that could put out records and be part of the scene, so I was much more involved.

It's crucial to be on the front line if you are running a record label. A maverick will always go where the action is. You have to have a nose and an instinct for the bands, but you also need a nose and an instinct for where the music scene is at, and in 1988 that scene was changing fast. Acid house was more than a night out; it was a lifestyle. Typically, I went in with both feet. It was everything that I had known about music turned upside down and inside out. That was one of the reasons why I liked it. If I'm honest, the other reasons were probably the drugs and the non-stop partying. My own life was also changing fast. Yvonne, my wife, had left me, and I don't blame her. I was going crazy at the time. After she left I moved down to Brighton and lived with Bobby Gillespie. That was always going to be crazy. We were going mental.

It was Innes who gave me my first tab of acid in 1988, and then I started taking ecstasy and that changed everything. We would go to clubs, buy the drugs, go back to my flat and take them and it was bonkers. I wasn't even that interested in the music for the first six months, it was just the ecstasy and what it made me feel like. Ecstatic. Literally.

I got into acid house later that year. I kind of stumbled into it. I was up in Manchester at the New Order/Happy Mondays gig at G-MEX in December 1988. I went to the party afterwards, which was in the basement of the Haçienda. There was a massive area under the club that stretched beneath the whole building. The post-gig party was billed as the E-Party, which kind of gave a clue as to what was going to be happening, and the night was known as Disorder, which was the state I would end up in. Typically and brilliantly of Factory, the party even had its own catalogue number – Fac 208.

The night was just the bands and the managers and their mates, and there weren't loads of people there. I remember only about seven people on the dance floor. I was on about three Es and there was a girl there called Hayley who I really liked, but I was so off my head that her head was turning into a green diamond, which I told her and I think scared her off. No surprise there. The party was an all-nighter and I was, of course, staying to the end. I was pilled up and I started dancing to the acid house records because I was so off my nut, and it was then that I thought... Fuck! I get it! I really get it. It was the first time I had taken the pill properly alongside the music in a club and it all suddenly made sense. I was a convert.

A few weeks later I moved up to Manchester and rented a flat above the Factory office in West Didsbury. Manchester was party central at the time. It really was Madchester. I would hang out with Shaun Ryder a lot, and he was the king of the scene. The whole city felt like it was off its head and it changed the way I felt about music. And life. Indie suddenly felt very old and boring and acid house was now the future. You have to have these epiphanies when you run a record label. It's a crime to be boring, and these obsessions and changes in direction keep you on your toes. Pop culture should never be a museum piece and you have to be ready to react to the sudden switches in direction. And after that night at the Haçienda, I became an acid house evangelist.

In the summer of 1989, we moved the Creation office from Hatton Garden to 8 Westgate Street in Hackney, and that's when things went up another level. We now brought the action to Creation. It was part office and part warehouse party, and because Hackney was a no-go zone then – nothing like it is now – no one would bother us so we went crazy. I got the whole office in London into the new scene, and we would have these weekend parties at the offices that were pure and totally mental.

The opening night of the new office would create a pattern for what followed. I invited music writers and any band I knew to the party and then turned them on to the new culture. These parties would change people's lives. We would just get hammered on ecstasy. It was like four or five pills handed out to each person, and the music would be pounding and gradually everyone would end up in this wild room on the top floor that was full of mirrors and with a glass roof, and in the end, most of them were sold on acid house.

At the end of each night, we would be dancing on the office roof, waiting for the sun to come up, all pilled up.

They were the craziest parties. Proper weekenders. The Valentines would come, Primal Scream would be there, people who worked in the office, accountants, nutters and pals. It was totally bonkers. I provided the stimulants. We'd be giving Es to everybody – the Es that I bought off the Happy Mondays didn't always work, but enough did. We were changing the culture of the label as well as the music scene around us. It infected us and then it infected the bands. It changed the way they sounded. It changed the way they looked. Primal Scream went from all-leather rock 'n' roll to a more casual look. It changed rock music and pop culture, and surely that's what a record label should be doing? You are out there and out of it and reporting back and bringing all this great music and culture back to the core and changing it all up. Cross-pollinating.

I put out some dance records as well and was going around the clubs in London, partying and immersing myself in this amazing new scene. The first dance record I released on Creation was Love Corporation's *Tones* in February 1990, on which Danny Rampling did a remix of 'Palatial', which was a killer track. We then released a whole bunch of dance twelve-inches, beginning with Fluke's 'Philly (Jamorphous Mix)', and Hypnotone's self-titled mini-album. Then there was an early indie/dance crossover of J.B.C.'s cover of The Rolling Stones' 'We Love You' – J.B.C. was The Jazz Butcher Conspiracy, the alias of a total genius from Northampton – and Sheer Taft's 'Cascades (Hypnotone Mix)', which was a project by this mad indie kid called Thomas Taft from Greenock near Glasgow who was making genius dance music.

People forget about Creation being a dance label but, for me, that was a really important part of what we did. The label was already unconventional, I suppose, but it became even more so. I would be off my face a lot – the whole office was – but we still got everything done. The workday would end and then it would turn into party central, and then the lines would get blurred and there would be lines on the desks. The courier would turn up with the drugs and we would start taking them. It was research, like buying singles had been when I was younger. Maybe. It was perfect for that time and we were right at the epicentre. Whatever was happening was happening right here.

Despite all this madness, I hadn't abandoned indie music. I still loved it. We had signed Ride to Creation in 1989, a bunch of teenage art school kids who I first heard via Cally Callomon, who worked at Warners and had signed an acid house project called The Grid that I was managing. He played me Ride's demo and I nodded along dutifully and gave nothing away but thought they sounded total genius – like the next generation My Bloody Valentine or The House of Love. I hoped Warners wouldn't sign them and went to speak to them. When you run your own label, you can move fast when you have to. Ride had all these big labels interested in them, but when this crazy guy goes to talk to them in his Glasgow accent it must have been disconcerting for a nice band from Oxford. Luckily they were fans of the label and maybe they liked my crazy attitude and so they signed to Creation instead of Warners. I think it made sense. A major label would have forgotten about them but they were a priority for us. They fitted in immediately, and far from being phased by the mad party scene going on around Creation, they joined in, so culturally they were in the right place on all levels! That's how to run a record label – have the best parties and put the best records out – and we managed to release their debut *Ride* EP in 1990 and it took off straight away.

We also signed Swervedriver around the same time, another brilliant group from Oxford, who ended up being one of our biggest bands in the USA, despite being lower on the radar in the UK.

So the indie guitar scene was still something that I was in touch with, but I was serious about the dance releases as well, and there were some really great ones. The dance bug started to infect the indie bands, too, and we had some remixes done that became classics. For me, that's how to run a record label – melding pop cultures and creating new hybrids, changing the sound of music and making great art that filled dance floors and took bands to really unlikely places. Bowie had done that with his records that I'd loved as a kid. And Primal Scream's radical transformation by Andy Weatherall's remodelling of 'I'm Losing More Than I'll Ever Have' into 'Loaded' was another perfect example. Then there was what many people consider the greatest remix of that scene, Weatherall's take on My Bloody Valentine's 'Soon', which contained extensive samples from WestBam's 'Alarm Clock' and rebuilt the song into something else entirely, whilst still keeping the magic and mystery of the original.

Acid house was huge and all-pervading but it has curiously been edited out of most pop culture narratives. It changed music and culture massively. Creation is testament to that. Maybe acid house's very nature, where the crowd was the star, makes it hard to signpost and document. Or maybe it was because everyone was too off their heads and having a good time to remember anything, or maybe the music was just too alien to most music media. But the scene turned music on its head as well as ushering in a whole new culture, style and drugs. For an avowed psychedelic fan like me, it made total sense.

By the end of 1989, I had moved from Manchester back to London, but acid house had changed everything. It was like punk rock in that it turned your life upside down. The drugs changed me and then I changed the label around. Turned it all upside down to see what came out.

PART TWO

Party Central

CHAPTER 8

······························

Stand your ground

I f you're going to start a business, you need to do it with someone who has all the talents that you don't. I may have ended up being the face of the label, but weirdly, initially, I was also the royalties and the business guy. That worked well at the beginning but, by 1991, when Creation started to get really big, there was a lot of money going through the label and my role changed. I ended up dealing with the personalities, the artists and the bands, and Dick Green started to deal with the business stuff, like the contracts and the fucking VAT man. That makes sense at a bigger label. The roles change, the priorities change, and you have to have someone like me who can deal with the dressing room like a Premiership football manager.

When we started, Dick was a 10 per cent shareholder in the label. We were actually quite organised on that level. We were these ludicrous little people who had somehow started a record label and a limited company but we sort of knew what we were doing. Then the label evolved and Dick evolved. He grew into it brilliantly – thank fuck! – because somebody needed to grow into it and to be my partner. At a certain point, I gave him a fair share of the money – half, instead of the two-thirds for me that it had originally been set up for. I couldn't have done the whole thing without him. I might have been the face of Creation but Dick deserved his money. Every band needs a frontman, but the frontman has to appreciate the rest of the band. You're just the face. They are the engine room.

For Dick to get into the business side was quite an ask for a guy who's pretty fucking gentle. Things could get quite hairy out there with the money stuff. Sometimes people would come to the office and say, 'Pay up or I'm going to break your fucking legs,' and threaten me over money. There was definitely still a criminal element around the edges of the music scene then. Stuff like that just brought out my worst behaviour, which meant I would literally physically throw them out of the office and down the stairs. It was always an advantage to have a Glasgow accent. I'd throw all the loonies out and tell them to 'get tae fuck'. People listened when I spoke Glasgow.

It was always a battle to survive. In the early days it was really hand to mouth, and then the Mary Chain took off and we had some breathing space. I think Dick was initially kinda shocked at the business side. I'm not surprised. I was more of a natural, from when I'd started managing The Jesus And Mary Chain, because they were the most dysfunctional people and I had to learn to deal with that side as well. They couldn't help it. I mean, they grew up like that, doing the music with just the two of them. Even at the start when I was saying let's do some records and pushing them along, it was almost five years of them being on the dole and not leaving their fucking house since they had first gone to London to try and make it before coming back to Glasgow and staying in to write songs. They had no idea of the real world and I had to make something happen. So we got the band busy and I put out their debut single, 'Upside Down'. I was the guy who said, I think I might need to put your record out on Creation. No one else was interested, but by then I knew the ropes from the first ten releases on the label and I had people in the music press and radio interested in what I was up to – we just needed a breakthrough. It was a different kind of standing your ground – when no one else is interested but your instinct tells you that you are right.

When they took off it was another type of standing your ground. I was still really naive at the time, but I knew my front would carry me through. I remember being in the Alaska Studios in London, which is where all the bands would rehearse at the time. A publisher had come down to check the Mary Chain out. I was talking to him about publishing, despite the fact that I knew next to nothing about it at the time, apart from the fact you got money. I didn't have a clue. Nobody we knew had a clue. So I was kinda blagging it, and I figured that maybe ten thousand pounds is what I should be effectively thinking to ask for whatever this publishing was. So we are talking and I'm doing my best to look like I know what I'm talking about. He goes, blah, blah, blah, money, and advances, and publishing this – and how much do you want? So I thought I would just try it on and I said sixty thousand quid for the publishing. He looked at me and said forty grand and that was it, done.

The three members of the Mary Chain had just moved to London and were living in band poverty hell in a one-room shithole bedsit flat in Fulham, so the deal got them all a nicer place to live. When I told them I had got them the money they thought I was a genius. So I realised at that point that I was onto something, that I could talk the talk and then walk the walk and then cash the cash. Also, as the manager, I had just made myself £8,000. I was fucking twenty-three years old and I was, like, that was really good. That's how it all works. It's a blag! I learned pretty quickly that you had to have the nerve to stand your ground in deals. You had to have the bottle to actually pitch for more than the band's worth and not be scared to ask.

I never thought we weren't gonna make money because I think I'm naturally fucking gifted at making cash, which is useful in this business. Saying that, I would also have been happy doing it for 100 quid a night, like when I DJ in Spain these days. It's like that when you are a proper music head. It's all great, like when Noel said he would have been just as happy being a roadie as being in Oasis. When I started, I always thought I would be on the fringes. That's what we're like. We all came from that world. We were outsiders looking in. Same with Noel or with Shaun Ryder or with Ian Brown – then when they did their fucking Wembley shows or something, they must have thought this is fucking mad. No one expects that level of success.

In the early years, Rough Trade looked after the label, but by the end of the eighties the wheels were coming off that. The indie underground was always a difficult world. You had a creative freedom but the money was always tight. Rough Trade distribution had been key to the early days of Creation, but they were in trouble. Before going bankrupt in 1991 they had changed the percentages on the distribution deal, as they were saying that they were managing stock and blah, blah, blah. And I was so fucking pissed off because I thought what they already charged was too high.

Rough Trade then started running into problems and the business got shorted when the distribution part went down, and then, effectively, we went out of contract. But just as we got out of the contract we started having big hits with Primal Scream's 'Loaded', My Bloody Valentine, and Ride's 'Chelsea Girl', and then suddenly, in 1990, the other big distributor – Pinnacle, who had always ignored us and who I hadn't really liked up to this point – showed interested in distributing Creation. I had loved the idea of Rough Trade's distribution, and they had given me a chance when I started – I will always be grateful to Geoff Travis for that – but I was a working-class guy from Glasgow, and they were middle class and that made a difference. In the indie world, Pinnacle were seen as the evil capitalists and Rough Trade as the cool socialists, even when they were putting up their cut to 29 per cent.

So a bidding war ensued between Pinnacle and Rough Trade for our distribution. The whole of Creation loved Rough Trade deep down because they were seen as having the indie ethics, but, because I was so annoyed with Rough Trade for putting up their percentage and the way they looked at us like we were chancers, so I played them off against each other and then I went to Pinnacle in 1990 and got a better deal and Rough Trade were fucked off with me and then went bust anyway.

For a couple of years that worked very well, but by 1992 the label was at a crossroads. We were having success with the bands but the money we were making was more than cancelled out by the costs of recording and manufacturing the records. We were running at a loss. It may be an asset to run a record label on instinct and enthusiasm but it doesn't make any business sense. Dick Green recognised this, but I was too far gone in my new chemical regime to notice or care. Eventually, we decided it might be a good idea to sell a share of the company. Just so that we could keep going.

Initially we had been speaking to Derek Green at China Records about selling him part of the label, and that had been going well until he told me that he was the managing director at A&M Records in 1977 when they had dropped the Sex Pistols during all the furore over 'God Save The Queen'. That was enough for me and I didn't do the deal, even though they were offering £2.5 million for Creation and we were desperate. It seems a crazy decision. It *was* a crazy decision, but I was still a mad punk rock kid and my mind was addled by the drugs. Still makes me laugh, though. The audacity!

At the time we owed Mayking Records a fortune. They were the company that manufactured all the records for us, and for nearly all the other indie labels at the time. We owed them £200,000, which was a hell of a lot for a small label. I'm trying to tell this next part of the story in a way that justifies our behaviour (well, my behaviour). We had started Creation from nothing, and someone who is now dead said, 'You're spending sixty to eighty grand a month on pressing records. If you don't pay for two months, that's one hundred and sixty grand that you can save, which you can make more records with and make some money maybe and pay them back further in the future.' I went 'Great idea – let's do that!' So we started paying late.

We had a good couple of years of that system until around 1992, when we started getting into debt because we were extending our credit. We would manufacture and keep pushing back the payments, but then we owed Mayking more than 200 grand that we would intend to pay fucking late. It's part of the gamble of running a label – being prepared to take these massive risks. A gamble with somebody else's money, really. Which is a bit naughty.

But anyway, the guy from Mayking got pissed off and he was a horror to deal with as well. I already really, really disliked him from back in 1980/81 when I was releasing The Laughing Apple records and I used to go into Mayking to manufacture them and he used to fucking have a go at me for being Scottish and take the piss out of my accent. That was a thing then, laughing at accents from outside London, like you were stupid. He would say stuff like, 'Aye, wee Scottish man,' and do all the crappy accents, and me being me and basically vulnerable and twenty and just off the train, that built up a lot of resentment inside me. At the time I was a wee guy in the business and I had to take it, but as I got bigger I realised he was a fucking clown.

Mayking had had enough, though, and put a stop to our account. In his new role, Dick had already had a few conversations with them in which they verbally beat him up about the money. In the middle of this, Derek Birkett from One Little Indian Records (who have now changed their name to One Little Independent Records following criticism of the original name) came down and tried to buy us out. Maybe Mayking who owned half of One Little Indian had sent him to see us, thinking we were so desperate that we would sell to anyone and that would clear the debt. Derek Birkett had set up One Little Indian to put out his anarchist punk band Flux of Pink Indians in the late seventies, and had built the label up to become one of the big indie labels at the time. They had the Sugarcubes and were doing well. They could have bought us out so I had to step in at that point and say I'd rather have gone bankrupt than give them the label. Derek Birkett came down to the bunker at Creation with his business affairs guy, Jay – who is a good guy – with this idea of a deal that was to basically carpet-bag my fucking business.

What they didn't know was that Sony were now also on the scene and offering me two and a half million pounds for Creation, and One little Indian didn't know that. I think they were offering £400,000. They thought that was a good deal and I let them detail it to me whilst I was sat there with Tim Abbot, who was now at Creation on the business side, trying to guess what I was going to do. The meeting got tense and it got shouty pretty quick between me and Derek Birkett. I was like, 'You're just a little fucking cunt.' Then I threw him out of the office, calling him a 'corporate whore'. He was supposed to be the fucking king of the fucking punks with his anarchist punk band background and he had literally just tried to steal somebody's fucking business! What was worse was that it was my busines

When I threw him out of the office I remember him shouting as he went through the door: 'Everybody says you've gone mad and you're on drugs...' That was funny, I'll give him that. And maybe true. Of course, it's different now. I'm not as mad as I was then. In many ways I think I've reverted back to 1982 fucking sober McGee. Being crazy helped in those days though, in the cut and thrust of how to run a record label. A lot of the time it was about survival. Standing your ground.

By then the only way we could survive was to try and get major labels involved. That's why I had been speaking to Sony. This was nothing new. I'd had dealings over the years with with the majors. In the early days of Creation I had set up an offshoot label called Elevation with Warners but it hadn't worked out and we had gone back to indie which was not easy. We were never a bedroom DIY label. The bigger the ambition the bigger the cost and we needed help to get to the next level. The stakes were a lot higher now. The bands were getting bigger and it was frustrating that we couldn't break bands like Primal Scream out across Europe. Thing is, we were totally on the tightrope. We needed investment.

Most indie labels like Creation only have one big band. If they are lucky. At that time ours was Primal Scream, and *Screamadelica* had been huge in the UK but its sales in Germany were not even a tenth of the UK sales. I knew the culture was different, but not that different. It was obvious that we needed a bigger machine behind us to get justice for these genius records. When you have bigger potential the stakes get higher. For every big band there may be a couple of other bands like Primal Scream who get past breaking even, and then a lot of bands who probably lose money. The music biz is insane. It's a crazy business model. The craziest. And it gets crazier if the big band takes a couple of years off and the cashflow from their 50:50 split stops – then the label has serious financial and cashflow problems.

Of course, when Creation got bigger and crazier there were a lot of hairy times in the office around money, and with bands just being fucking booze and drug-addled rock stars. There were lots of mad people who decided they would make our lives a fucking misery. That was where someone like Ed Ball was a really important part of the team. Ed didn't make money but he did keep us afloat with his warm nature. He not only made some great records for us, either solo or as Love Corporation, but he also had that feelgood thing that is key at a record label. When things got mad or tense, he would float in with a big warm bear hug and calm everything down. There can be a lot of stress in a place like that, and a lot of fragile people, so you need someone who can make the vibe good. Whilst there was me being me, all manic and crazy, and Dick stressing and making money, Ed kept the fucking vibe up. I think that's pretty important. Crucial. You hundred per cent need that at a record label.

By then Dick was the business guy, and probably the meat and potatoes guy. Someone had to run the ship. When there was a big deal to be done, I would do it, but it was crucial that there was someone to do the day-to-day, dotting the 'i's and getting the basics right, who was also a music person. That was Dick. Joe Foster was part of the inner core as well. He was the producer, ideas guy and tastemaker. It was an unlikely team. Music nuts in control of a runaway ship.

Maybe we needed someone else who was more audacious than all of us?

Which is why I had brought in Tim Abbott, who I met in the madness of the acid house days. He had been doing marketing for people like Levi's. He was less indie than we were and a proper entrepreneur, and when he came on board things changed a lot. I'd met him when the label was doing really well and we were in our boom years, but somehow I wasn't earning anything out of it. I was putting all my money back into the label and it was like a bottomless pit – like with New Order and the Haçienda. That was how it was then – big ideas seemed more important than feeding yourself. I wasn't taking a wage from Creation. I thought that was how you ran a label. That was punk rock. The bands were getting all the big deals and doing ok, and I was taking nothing. I hadn't realised that I could get paid properly as well until I got Tim on board.

Tim became a key part of the inner core and he changed a lot of things around, getting us much more business orientated. He was as mad as me and lived the same sort of lifestyle, and he also made things happen. Running a record label the way I did it, in a 24/7 rock 'n' roll way, was a lonely business. No one could keep up with me. Not until Tim Abbot. He wasn't always popular with everyone at Creation because of this but, for me, he was vital to the label.

Initially, he was this funny little guy that I had met in Birmingham when I had moved up there in 1990 with my then partner Belinda McConnell. I was there only at weekends, trying to sober up from the mad weeks in London. One weekend in 1991, me and Bobby Gillespie had gone up to Birmingham to see Saint Etienne play a Heavenly Recordings night with the Manic Street Preachers. Tim was promoting the gig and we all ended up at his house afterwards. It was one of those typically mad nights when the Es came out; a snapshot of the way the music business was in those days – well, my corner of it anyway – before it all got a bit too slick and pro. We were doing loads of coke and Es and he was coming up with all these business strategies and tacky marketing ideas that somehow made real sense to me in terms of Creation. We hit it off immediately. He not only had these great ideas but he also knew where to get the best pills in 1991, which wasn't so easy by then. This was how to run a record label!

He was already in the business running a club called The Better Way, and it dawned on me pretty quick that we needed someone like him at the label. And it wasn't just the coke doing the talking. He came round to my place in London one night and we were on the coke again and he started to ask me about my own finances. He had come down to London to help do an audit for us, which was already a bit weird as we never bothered with that kind of thing, which was why the label's finances were in chaos. He asked what I did with the money and I told him I just put it all back in the label and he told me that was certainly *not* how to run a record label. He pointed out that the business model of Creation was all wrong – that I was running it like a fan and not as a business, and that needed sorting for my own sake and more importantly for the label's sake. In all that madness he was talking real sense. And I was listening. He was right about it being a problem when you are involved in a passion career – you lose sight of the finances, and it's crucial to be aware of that. Because we were involved in the extreme end of showbiz, and we were living it and not thinking about the rest of our lives, we were making problems for ourselves down the line.

I quickly moved Tim into Creation and into the bunker. It freaked everyone in the office out when this mad whirlwind appeared from nowhere. I think they all thought he was my drug buddy. He might well have been, but he also did a great job of turning the label around. There was me and him in the bunker with our sex and drugs and rock 'n' roll, and Dick with his flow charts. It might have looked a bit crazy but it worked. I felt sorry for Dick having to put up with the pair of us – we were lunatics running riot. The speed at which we were going was insane, but somehow we made it work. Pop culture was fast forward in the early nineties and we were going even faster.

Not that Tim coming on board meant everything became more conventional. He may have talked business sense but he was even madder than the rest of us. In many ways, he was not just my business partner but my partner in crime. We would forever be in LA doing an outrageous amount of drugs and chasing women. This was before Tim cleaned up in 2003. We were way more rock 'n' roll than any of the bands, yet somehow, in the middle of this madness, Tim was coming up with these great marketing ideas and making me realise that we needed to get the label on a proper business footing.

When he came in he saved the arse of the company. Because he was coming from the outside he could see things that we were too close to or that we were too attached to. One of the first things he did was look at the figures and tell me that we should drop My Bloody Valentine. The band were costing me financially and emotionally but I couldn't see the wood for the trees. Once Tim called it, it all made sense and in January 1992 I rang Kevin and told him I was dropping him from the label. He was in shock. It had never occurred to him the effect that all the stress and the financial and emotional drain was having on me. Mind you, within twenty-four hours every label in the UK was fighting to sign

My Bloody Valentine, and Island gave them half a million pounds for an album that didn't appear for years.

Sometimes when you run a label you have to make these kinds of decisions. The artist may be a genius but the situation was out of control. Kevin and I didn't really speak for years. We fell out over an interview in a magazine where he said stuff about me, and me being from Glasgow I had to reply. Fortunately, we made up years later, following the *Upside Down* film about Creation in 2010. I loved his band and his records, and I was grateful Creation got to release them, but I was even more relieved that I never got caught in the matrix of trying to make the third album! I just couldn't cope with the way he made them. Twenty-one years later the new album finally came out, and of course *m b v* is another work of genius, and the way he released it online, crashing his own website, was brilliant. But I would have been bankrupt and would have had a full-on breakdown if I'd waited that long.

The mad thing was, the deeper we got into the drugs, the more professional the label was getting. The thing is, running a record label is a delicate balancing act. It's about dealing with flaky people and rip-off merchants, and it's about surviving the years when the money doesn't come in. It's about finding the money to create the space to make stuff happen. And there comes a time for every independent label when it has to make its mind up just what it is. You have to decide whether your label is a hobby or if you are a serious player. Some purists will call it 'selling out', but they have little idea of what it takes to make a label work and also the cost and work needed to break the kind of bands that we had. To market the bands properly and do them any justice, you need a big label behind you.

The finances were also always on a knife edge because we were trying to have fair deals with the bands. The way we would work with every band was in that time-honoured indie label way of giving them a 50:50 deal that we copied from Factory Records. These were the sort of deals where you split the profits from the records between the label and the band, which on paper seems to be the fairest way of doing it. The trouble is that it doesn't work if you are trying to run an indie label. The margins were really tight and the wolf was never far from the door.

In the end, Sony bought 49 per cent of the label for two and a half million in September 1992 and we were saved. If the deal had not worked out we would have gone bust. Those kinds of deals always seemed to be 51:49. I guess it looked good and made us feel like we were still in control. The deal also made me a millionaire, just as I had promised myself when I started on this mad journey. Now that's how to run an indie label!

Hunter S. Thompson described the music business as 'a cruel and shallow money trench, a long plastic hallway where thieves and pimps run free, and good men die like dogs. There's also a negative side.' And he was correct. Running a label is not only about standing your ground for your artists, but also standing your ground against artists who go too far, or managers who demand too much, or the various sharks that swim in the same sea. Ultimately, though, a big part of running a record label is holding your nerve in a crisis. I think I got away with it, and we somehow survived and thrived.

With Tim, things just got too much for me, and having a best mate who was madder on the drugs than I was, was not doing either of us any good. After my breakdown in 1994, Tim just kept going. After Creation, he went on to have his own career, managing Robbie Williams and lots of other stuff. Apart from the bonkers stuff, though, his time at the label was crucial for me, and he guided Creation towards a less shambolic approach and stopped us from being a typical indie label, getting us on a proper grounding with a deal with Sony. God knows how he managed it. God knows how I managed it!

CHAPTER 9

....

The importance of mentors

C reation didn't come out of a vacuum, and there were plenty of people that inspired me on my journey. There were the game-changing bands and musicians that I loved, like Bowie and the Sex Pistols when I was younger. When I found out about the classic managers, like Andrew Loog Oldham who looked after The Rolling Stones I realised then that it wasn't just the bands that shaped pop culture, it was the managers and the record label bosses too, and their ideas and the way they disrupted the status quo fascinated me.

It wasn't always the flash, dangerous managers and the big characters that were mentors to me. There were others who may not have initially fit that picture. When it got to the nuts and bolts of creating a label, I have to say – even if I want to fucking punch myself for it – that being around Rough Trade distribution and Geoff Travis made them my mentors as well in a way. They taught me so fucking much.

Their take on the music business was so different. It wasn't from the brash school of the music biz. It was more of a socialist culture. I don't think things are like that anymore. That was the left-wing nature of post-punk in the late seventies. When we were starting out and just down from Glasgow, politically we felt like we had an empathy with these ideals, even if Rough Trade was ultimately probably a wee bit too middle class for us. In the end, though, they encouraged me to make records and start a label, and they made me realise that you didn't have to come from comfy Chelsea or be West London posh to be involved in music. It was for normal people too. That was really important.

Rough Trade distribution was vital, and you have to hand it to Geoff Travis for creating it because it was a work of genius. They came up with a system that got those DIY records out around the country. They opened the doors to all those mad little labels that appeared after punk and were encouraged by John Peel playing their records. They were post-punk mentors for kids like us. Rough Trade taught me the basics of running a label, from the business side to the practical side of making the records, because being there in their warehouse and around lots of fucking people talking like they did was an education. Rough Trade distributed Creation from 1983 to 1991 and we learned so much in that time. They gave me a chance. I can respect that.

I remember one time in the early days, when Creation was really in trouble. There was a guy called Pete Walmsley who was the Rough Trade distribution guy. At the time I hated CDs, and all our early Creation albums were on vinyl. Pete suggested we make 300 CDs of each album and sell them in Japan only, as they love CDs there and we would be able to pay off our debt. So we did, and it worked. It was great advice. It was all about how to find these nooks and crannies to get your music out there and make small pots of money to survive. It was a great time to be around people like that who knew the ropes. They were older guys who knew all the tricks, and they were a real help.

Creation had a bumpy start, but you learn so much more from failure than you do from success. So for all those early years that we failed, we were learning. We didn't have any proper success until 1984 and The Jesus And Mary Chain's first single, but being around Rough Trade during the various failures of the first three or four years was a crash course in how to run a label. That was monumental and built our foundations and made Rough Trade a really important mentor for me.

When we started out, the only money we had came from the gigs I was putting on at The Living Room nights in London, and that was invested in making the records. Ironically, when The Jesus And Mary Chain blew up, the label almost imploded because it was so hard to keep up with the pressing of the records; we weren't built for success. We were such a bedroom DIY operation at the time that paying for each pressing before the money had come back in almost caught us out. Luckily our Rough Trade mentors were good for advice and helped us through that period as there was no road map.

In a very different way, Tony Wilson was also a massive early mentor for me. He had done a remarkable job at Factory Records. The concept for the label was so clever and the music was mind-blowing. The Factory artwork also looked great – all of it – those great Peter Saville sleeves created a real aesthetic. Like a northern Malcolm McLaren, Tony knew his pop culture and the media and he saw the bigger picture. He made everyone stay in Manchester instead of moving to London, which was what people always used to do when they made it, and he turned the city around with music. That was fucking amazing. He was very opinionated and he was also my friend. I remember meeting him in 1984 at a gig in Manchester, backstage at the Haçienda, and we got on straight away. Later, when I met him again, Tony said to me, 'Why do you keep trying to sell your bands to majors? You've just done that with the Mary Chain. If you stop selling your bands to majors then you will get much more money and you can build the label.' He was right, of course. It was better for the label and it was also better for the bands.

The way Tony and I talked about each other in the press, you would have thought we were rivals, but that was all part of the game. I think Tony Wilson liked me, but I don't think he respected me, but then he was ten years older than me and he was one of my heroes, not the other way round, and that's ok with me. I am not knocking him in any way, because I loved Tony. He was a hero and a mentor.

People from our punk and post-punk world are like indie thinkers. We are independent people. It wasn't just about the money for us, it was who we were as people, and that wasn't always easy for the bands who often wanted to sign to majors. If The House of Love had stayed on Creation for a few more years then they would have had a totally different career because we really got what they were about and they would have been a priority for us. We wanted them to stay on Creation. They were a brilliant band and I wanted them to be massive. I really believed in them, and I'm convinced we could have achieved that with Creation, which would have been good for all of us, but they wanted to sign to a major, which I understand, of course. If you are in a band you want stability to be creative, and the madness of an indie label is not easy to cope with. But they seemed to get lost on the bigger label and they just sort of disappeared into the machine. It was a big lesson. I don't blame them for going, I just wish they had stayed in our mad gang.

Tony Wilson saw through all of that. He saw the big picture. It was about a cultural revolution for him, about keeping hold of the music and the bands and changing the way things were done. He was more of an ideas person than me and was always ahead of the game. It was more than releasing records for him. He already had the Haçienda, and a few years later he was into MP3s and digital music before anyone else knew what it was. He was always peering into the future, whereas I've just always been a music fan, and that's what keeps me going, even today.

Malcolm McLaren was amazing. A real mentor. He was there for me as well. For someone who had grown up with punk, Malcolm was such a big deal. He was the manager of the Sex Pistols and had started the punk revolution for fuck's sake! He was the provocateur. He had the plan and the theories.

He started punk, I guess. He was a big figure that I looked up to. When we became friends in about 1995/96, it was a big thing for me. I first met him at a *Punch* magazine interview that we did together. Oddly, Malcolm was quite nervous of me. I was the one who seemed confident but deep down I was really nervous of him and it made for quite a spiky interview. I said a few things I didn't really mean and I kinda won the interview battle without meaning to. One question that Malcolm was asked was what would you do if you had Oasis, and he had a benign polite answer, and then I was asked what I would do if I had the Sex Pistols and I said I would not have let them break up, and that if I was in control of them they would have been the biggest band in the world.

Unbelievably, despite that interview, we became pals. Being pals with Malcolm was like a proper education. We would meet up once a month, sometimes once a week, and go for a meal. I liked the idea of how we could just talk through everything, from music, pop culture, streaming or whatever he was obsessed by, which could be China, tribal culture, politics, style or MP3s, and then how it all joined together. He would talk at all kinds of tangents and it was always inspiring.

By the time I met him he felt that rock 'n' roll was all square and that 'all we have now is rock 'n' roll collectors', which he would sneer in that distinctive voice. He looked way beyond the music at all of culture, politics and art. I was just a music guy but Malcolm knew how to complete the whole pop culture picture, and because he knew this he also knew how to tear the fabric. He had a whole lot of culture in his head. For him, every single thing that was going on had a pop art reason behind it. He was fascinated with the future and the internet and MP3s which were then like a sci-fi glimpse into what was coming, and it would eventually inspire me to set up my post-Creation label Poptones, which was all online. The trouble with Malcolm was that he was so far in the future with his ideas that even when I did the downloads label a couple of years later, after his inspiration, I was still too far ahead of most people and the label didn't really work.

My thing was on a different level than Malcom's, in that I was a music fanatic. I was actually genuinely fascinated by bands and rock 'n' roll records. I don't think Malcolm was like that. It was the culture that interested him. As much as I aspired to be like that, I just wasn't a cultural provocateur. People say that maybe I was with Britpop, but I think it happened despite me. I felt a strong affinity with punk and acid house – those were my things – and by the time it got to Britpop, I was too old. For me, it was actually a load of nonsense, with people running around in Union Jacks.

* * *

Another mentor I learned a lot from was The Rolling Stones' manager in the sixties, Andrew Loog Oldham, who is a fucking genius. Of all these guys, he was the first. He invented the concept of the young manager who took it beyond the music and was not scared to cause trouble. Malcolm, Tony Wilson and Seymour Stein – who set up Sire and signed The Ramones, The Undertones, Madonna and many others – were all game-changers who came after Andrew had changed the way things were done and created the visionary blueprint of the manager who created the full picture. When he took over the management of The Rolling Stones in 1963, he changed the band. He made them the bad boys, in contrast to The Beatles' clean-cut image. He put the focus on Mick Jagger and away from Brian Jones, and made them more pop with a rebel edge, instead of blues purists. He not only produced them but was creative in their whole image. Basically, he made the Stones into something they weren't, into rebels, and that sold them to the public. He came up with these brilliant slogans, like 'would you let your daughter marry one of The Rolling Stones', touching a raw nerve in the stuffy post-war UK.

I first met Andrew Loog Oldham when I was DJing in Mexico City in 2006. The meeting was set up through Joe Foster who somehow knew him. Because I was staying over in Mexico City kicking my heels for a couple of weeks after

DJing, I invited Andrew to fly out to meet me because he lived in Bogota with his superstar model wife. So he came out to see me and we were talking and hanging out and got on like a house on fire. It was a wild weekend. He told me that by the time he was twenty-six he had done it all. That's how fast things went in the sixties. A lot of those guys made it really young and got to the other side before they were even thirty. You forget that, because these days everyone in the music biz is older and things take longer to happen. In the sixties the culture was so new and youthful and it was in fast forward. When Andrew was managing the Stones he was actually younger than they were. He was just a kid, barely twenty, the same age as the audience. He just got in the fast lane and did it all. He had the ideas and he turned the Stones from students into rebels.

For me, Andrew is one of the main movers. He had the magic touch. He knew the best bands and how to make them sound better and seem cooler. He was musical as well. Not only did he shape and mould the bands, he sometimes produced them. His background was in PR so he knew how to play the press, shaping and molding the band's image and the music. His hero was Phil Spector so he was obsessed with creating a British wall of sound along with his very British wall of media hype. By doing this he changed the course of music. He's the guy that made Jagger and Richards write songs by locking them in a kitchen and refusing to let them out until they had a song. He said to them, 'I want a song with brick walls all around it, high windows and no sex.' And then clicked the door shut. The song they came up with was 'As Tears Goes By' and was a big hit for Marianne Faithfull. That's a great way of doing A&R. Sometimes you just have to take drastic action and make it happen. You don't fuck about. Not so much mothers lock up your daughters as managers lock up your band into the fucking kitchen.

Seymour Stein was another key figure for me. He had been around since the beginning of rock 'n' roll and had an amazing roster of bands. He had a golden period in the seventies and into the eighties with his label Sire Records, signing the Ramones and Talking Heads in 1975, The Pretenders in 1980 and Madonna in 1982. He also signed The Replacements, Depeche Mode, The Smiths, The Cure, Ice-T, Ministry, The Undertones, Echo and the Bunnymen and many more. He had great taste and the bands he signed were game-changers. He was good to me as well and gave me brilliant advice, like with the Sony deal for Creation when that came up in 1992.

The advice I was getting from my mentors was key to the whole deal. I was in talks with Derek Green at China and I asked Seymour for advice, and he said that if you work with an independent then you get half the pie, but with some majors you are the crumbs and they won't even notice, so you are better in the indie world. But he also said that Sony would be different. That they would let you be you. At the time it was either Sony or China Records. China were ambitious and buying up other labels, but Seymour said don't go with Derek Green because he will try and change you from day one. So I used China's interest as a card to play with Sony. It was brilliant advice from Seymour.

Ironically, I didn't get Seymour when I first met him because I was young and hadn't sussed him out. Initially I thought he was just part of the corporate world. We got off to a bad start when we first met at Cannes, when he came up to me and said, 'It's the new Brian Epstein.' I took it badly, probably because I was feeling bad about myself, or something wasn't right in my personal life, and then this successful guy was laughing at me and that screwed me out. But when I had the Valentines he really started to show his hand and how amazing he was. At first when he wanted to sign them I stalled him for a year. I wouldn't take his calls. This went on for months, but then we needed the money and I answered. Once he had signed them and we got to know him, it was totally different. An eye-opener. He was a guru to me and we ended up being amazing friends. We were rolling and he was fucking brilliant and we signed Ride,

Primal Scream and My Bloody Valentine to him to put out in the States.

Seymour was a fucking legend. He had a great story on everyone, from the bands he signed to the people he nearly signed, like Jimi Hendrix. The music never stopped with him; he just carried on until he died. He was as hip to doo-wop as he was to the latest dive bar band. He was an encyclopaedia of pop culture and an inspiration, and you need mentors like that to keep you going in the music business.

CHAPTER 10

....

What defines a great record

The key to running a record label is to know what a great record is – or at least bluff that you do – but it's not as easy as it looks. The attempt to define a great record has sparked a billion debates in pubs, clubs, gigs and across the internet for decades. For some, there are core formulas to create a perfect song or a great pop artefact but, for me, it's a split second of just knowing and being certain of your intuitive power. I spent my teenage years immersed in records. I bought every hit record regardless of genre, and listened so much that it might be in my DNA by now without me even knowing.

To be honest, it's not even that rock 'n' roll – I was, and still am, like Bobby Gillespie, a total record geek. We were not wild rock 'n' rollers. We were record collectors. I started with glam and loads of other styles of music, and then got really into it with seven-inch punk rock singles. This was my education and how I saw the world.

In the mid-seventies, I was obsessed with Bowie. Then a lot of the kids like me got into punk and were buying punk records. Punk might have been year zero for the media, where you were not meant to like anything before that, but David Bowie got a pass. He was so good and his shadow was so long over everything that no one dared to try and take Bowie out of it. It was not the same for everyone, though. I still liked Bob Dylan but suddenly it seemed as though he was from a different time zone so I got rid of his records. That was the trick of the time. It's embarrassing to say so now but a few weeks before, he was really cool, but now he seemed really old-fashioned. As soon as the year zero idea was over and you could like the music you really liked again, I started buying my old records back. It took me a few years to get all the Bob Dylan albums back but it was worth it. Those years of collecting records taught me a lot. I was so immersed in music that I knew what I wanted. And if you are truly into running a record label you need to be steeped in music and the culture and the lifestyle.

Sometimes a great record can be something that you have never really heard before, like 'Upside Down' by The

Jesus And Mary Chain and 'Supersonic' by Oasis, and it gives you the shock of the new and that is part of the thrill. They may have something that bands were doing before, but not in the same way that they are doing it, and that difference is crucial. Oasis's 'Supersonic' is a twist on their version of Madchester, except it's heavier and with more guitars. It's almost like a kind of rock classic in the amount of guitars and an almost metal version of baggy. It's like the rock version of that whole scene. Or, to be more accurate, it's like putting Madchester through a fuzzbox. And a shitload of compression. When Shaun Ryder first heard 'Supersonic' he said that for him it sounded like a heavy metal version of the Mondays and he knew it was going to be massive. And he was right. On both counts.

The Jesus And Mary Chain may have been doing their take on Doctor Mix And The Remix, this weird French band and a side project of Métal Urbain, who used a cheap drum machine and made a great rock 'n' roll noise on their cult album of covers of The Stooges and the Velvets and their own stuff. What was cool about the Mary Chain was that they did this in their own way and not in the same way as the original. It's that difference that creates a unique spin on something, even if the artist themselves is not trying to be unique and is often totally unaware of it. 'Upside Down' was the seven-inch that sent Creation soaring. When you run a label you are waiting. Waiting for the moment. Waiting for the song. Waiting for the band. I had some good early releases but I needed that defining record. It's hard to say how, but you know it's going to come and that you'll just know it when you hear it. And 'Upside Down' was that moment.

A record like that may sound effortless but that alchemy is almost impossible to create. It was a perfect cross between the fury of the post-punk underground and the wistful classic melodies of late sixties dark pop. It was this meld of punk and psychedelia into something that sounded so fresh and new that it sparked a revolution and set a template for the label's future. In a way, my job at the record label was to spot that unique spin. To be aware of it or sometimes to pull it out of the band or even create it for the band. Create the space and make it happen.

What makes a great band is to have the vision to just do that. Just do it. What makes a great record label is being aware of it. What makes a great manager is to keep your phone charged! With a great record it's that 5 per cent twist that counts. Nothing is completely original that has ever been massively successful. It's always been a warped version of something else. That warp is everything. With the label, I used to get involved in the process to find that mystical 5 per cent warp that made a good song great. As I get older I do much less of that. That's more of what I get Youth from

Killing Joke, now one of the biggest producers in the world, to bring to the table when he produces my bands. I take it to that kind of person to finish off or add a twist and make a good record great. Putting people with the right producers is a key part of what I do now as a manager and what I used to do as a record label.

Maybe I've always been in pursuit of the great record. When I was younger I was listening to records and subconsciously trying to work out what the magic was. As I have got older I'm not sure I know anymore what works. I know about old bands and what they are going for and what they should and shouldn't do and what they should sound like, but I have no idea about younger bands these days. There is an argument among some people that old records are better than new records – I'm not sure if I agree, but on the other hand, in modern rock 'n' roll there is no Jimi Hendrix type figure, is there? Maybe the role of music has changed, making the role of a record label almost redundant.

For one thing, we are living in a different culture now. In the old days of the label, most of the bands wrote their own songs. The bands were self-contained and you had to hope that somewhere in their tightly sealed unit someone knew what they were doing and how to write great songs. These days creativity exists beyond the band and everyone collaborates. It can either be the band collaborating with outside people for their own music, or writing with other people on different projects. A guy like Kyle Falconer from The View is a prime example of this. He is always in America these days, writing songs with and for other people as much as being in his own band. The next generation have such a different way of working. If Noel Gallagher was of this period he would be collaborating too, but when he came through he didn't need to do that because he was so successful anyway and the approach to being in a band was so different.

In a way, Primal Scream were innovators because they always collaborated – even decades ago. They worked with so many different people to achieve what they were aiming for. They ended up collaborating with Björn Yttling, the Swedish producer who was in Peter Bjorn and John, and who had produced and written songs with Chrissie Hynde, Franz Ferdinand, Sahara Hotnights and many others. It's something Primal Scream have always done from day one, when they collaborated with Clive Langer on their debut *Sonic Flower Groove* album. Then, of course, it was famously Andy Weatherall on their classic *Screamadelica* album, which was the ultimate collaboration. They were ahead of the game in that respect – now it's normal and commonplace for bands to do this.

What makes a great record changes all the time. That's part of the fascination for me. It could be a classic pop seven-inch single, it could be a perfect melody, or it could simply be something that sounds amazing. What makes a great record would change for us all the time. We started out as a pop art label doing pretty much what the Television Personalities were already doing. It was all very punk rock pop art psychedelic or punk psychedelia, as I call it. Then I broke The Jesus And Mary Chain who were a bit more punk rock I suppose. After that, I was releasing all these noisier bands, like Meat Whiplash or The Membranes, to try and target an audience.

When we ran into Kevin Shields and signed My Bloody Valentine it took the label into shoegazing before it was even invented. I would argue that the Valentine's period was the best-ever period of the label in terms of the bands that we had across the whole roster. We signed Slowdive, Swervedriver, Moonshake, Adorable and lots of that stuff. Oddly, when we signed them, Slowdive felt like a fringe band for us, who we thought would do great after My Bloody Valentine. They made a couple of great albums with us but for most music fans who were between Madchester and Britpop they were untrendy, and apart from a core of fans, nobody gave a fuck about the albums, you couldn't give them away. But two decades later, when they reformed, they headlined to 20,000 people at Primavera Sound festival in Barcelona. Back then, it wasn't cool to be middle class, not like now where it's really difficult to be working class in music. And Slowdive were middle class, nice kids and a great band. They were all about sixteen years old when I signed them in the back of a pub in Windsor. They were fans of The House of Love and Ride and were really influenced by the Valentines – like the next generation of that sound already. They were very good when we signed them and they did ok, but they were swamped by Oasis and Britpop. Now everyone has caught up with them and they have become massive in the last few years. Maybe that shows that a great record can also be about timing.

All the time my tastes were changing, and what would have been the perfect record for me ten years ago has changed over time. At one period I would have been obsessed with The Jesus And Mary Chain, and then I would have been obsessed with My Bloody Valentine. When I had the Valentines and Slowdive I launched, by mistake, a whole scene that the music press called shoegazing – maybe that was Creation's moment, when we really did start something and, in many ways, were driving the music scene with the bands that we were releasing. It was the closest we had come to creating a genre, even if it was Kevin Shields who really started it.

People always pointed at us and blamed us for other things that happened – things that were nothing to do with us. At one point, looking back in the mid-nineties, I got blamed for C86, the wave of Mary Chain bands, twee indie bands, indie dance and Britpop. I got the blame for all of that and often have to think maybe we were to blame because, maybe, we were leading the music scene at the time rather than reacting to it. Ironically, when Britpop happened I didn't sign too many Oasis-sounding bands apart from Heavy Stereo, whose singer Gem Archer ended up joining Oasis, and a couple of other bands like that. Maybe I should have signed more because that would have been my chance to cash in on myself!

All those different waves of bands were big parts of the Creation story, and with each wave we would try to define and redefine the perfect record. That's the key thing in pop culture. It's never static, and just when you think you have got it pinned down it's moved somewhere else. You just have to move with it or remain with what you know, or sometimes you hope to start a movement. For a good fifteen years or more I was ahead of the game and I could feel what was going on. From punk rock to acid house, I was in the middle of it, and to be part of two of the craziest scenes in British pop culture was pretty exciting.

CHAPTER 11

....

The art of discovery
– and going supernova

The nights that change your life are never the ones you are expecting, are they? I was in Glasgow in 1993 and it was my birthday, so I'd arranged to meet my sister at a Creation night at King Tut's, headlined by two of the newer bands we had signed who were from Glasgow – 18 Wheeler and Boyfriend.

I had gone down there early because Debbie Turner was playing with her band, Sister Lovers. Debbie is one of the coolest people I think I've ever met. She was really wild but also really smart and really knew her music. I had met her a few years previously and hung out with her a lot in Manchester. She is an amazing person. I walk into the venue and the night is running later than I thought and it was not even open yet. I look over the room and there is some band that she's brought up from Manchester in the back of her van hanging about. I remember this amazing-looking kid who had a blue tracksuit on. I thought he must be the drug dealer because bands at that time always had a cool-looking drug dealer with them. I didn't know it then but that was Liam. As they were setting up, I had a chat with Debbie and then went upstairs to meet my sister and get a few drinks.

Before the bands went on I was talking to Gerry Love from Teenage Fanclub, who's a good guy but I was not up for a long conversation, so when somebody shouted down the stairs 'That band's coming on, McGee,' I ran up the stairs just for a break from the chat. Oasis were coming on and they played 'Rock 'N' Roll Star' and it sounded great. I was really surprised and thought, who the fuck is this? I was thinking maybe the next song will be rubbish but it was 'Bring It On Down' and that was great as well. Then it was 'Up In The Sky', and I was already signing them in my head. This was a band I could release, but I was also aware that I was quite drunk and maybe they were not as good as I was thinking they were. Then Liam goes, 'This one is the Beatles song "I Am the Walrus",' and I was thinking that this was the bit where they fall down because no one can cover a Beatles song better than the original, but it was a brilliant version.

At that point I was like, fantastic, I must sign these. So when the set ended I went up to their sound guy, who turned out to be Mark Coyle, who I knew because he had just recently been sacked by Teenage Fanclub for hanging out with me, which they thought distracted me from looking after them! I said to Coyley, 'Who's the manager?', and he said 'There is no manager,' because this was before Marcus Russell had even got the gig with them. So I said, 'Who's the leader of the band?' Coyley said he would go backstage and get him and he comes back a few minutes later with Noel Gallagher, who comes trotting down the stairs with a cassette in his hand. On the spot I asked him if he wanted a record deal and he said who with? Looking back, I'm not sure if he was playing me or if he didn't know who I was. Maybe he was just being cute. I suspect he didn't know it was me at that moment, but then he said 'Are you Alan McGee?'

The mad thing about Noel Gallagher is how good his memory is to this day. I don't really remember what I was wearing that night, yet when he tells this story he remembers exactly what I was wearing. Every fucking detail. He tells people I was wearing red shoes, white Levi's, a green jacket, had a skinhead, and I looked like I had been on acid for two fucking years – and that's not that far off!

Maybe I was on their horizon, I don't know. People mention the life-sized cardboard cut-out promo of me, which was in Debbie's flat. Liam had been round to Debbie's before the gig and seen the cardboard cut-out and said, 'Who's that weird cunt!' So I was on some sort of horizon, I guess. And Coyley knew me really well of course. He must have gone upstairs and said to Noel, 'Alan McGee is out there and he is raving about your band,' instead of 'There's some random bloke out there who likes your band.'

I think I got there just at the right moment, though. I was actually late to this party because Oasis had been around a couple of years maybe, playing average shows, and I could have missed out on that magic moment when it all came together. When I saw them they were at the top of their game and I totally saw it. After the gig, when I met Noel, I liked him straight away. He had been hustling since he was fifteen. That was his thing. When I signed him at twenty-five, he was at his hustling peak. This was his moment. And mine. But I know now that there was a feeling in Manchester that Oasis had already missed the boat. Their big chance had come when they supported this band called Sweet Jesus at the Boardwalk in Manchester in August 1991, when there was a punch-up on stage. Sweet Jesus were the buzz band at the time. Geoff Travis had signed them to Rough Trade and their sort of glam indie was like early Britpop. All the other record companies were there that night and Oasis were doing their first-ever gig as the support band. They were third on the bill. It was before Noel was even in the band. He was in the crowd watching the gig and they put the ball over the bar. They had an argument on stage and completely blew it, but it was early days.

Somebody also told me that Caroline Elleray, who was a Manchester-based A&R person and had managed bands like World of Twist and Intastella, and who went on to sign Coldplay, was helping the early Oasis out. She had got a few music biz people to show up for this gig way before I ever saw them. It was like this showcase for London labels to see some bands and they all came up and they all passed on Oasis. Nobody talks about that because that's almost worse than Decca turning down The Beatles!

When the band played in Glasgow that night, I had no idea who they were and thought I had never met Noel before. When I think about it now, though, there are a few interesting bits to the story that make me realise that we were in a sort of long-distance orbit of each other. Before Glasgow, in 1992, we had signed Bob Mould from Hüsker Dü's new band, Sugar, and they were playing the Boardwalk in Manchester. Debbie came to the gig with me and said let's have a fucking crafty fucking wee spliff in her rehearsal room, which was downstairs because beneath the venue there were all these rooms where Happy Mondays, A Certain Ratio and The Membranes rehearsed. So we went downstairs and I sat in this rehearsal room and I looked around the room and saw a fucking Union Jack painted on the wall. She said Oasis had painted it, as they shared the room, and I asked are they fascists because of the flag thing, and she joked yeah, and laughed. That was the first time I must have been aware of them, even though the name didn't register, probably because I was so stoned and only interested in chatting with Debbie. Then there was another time at the Boardwalk, when I was in the rehearsal room with Medalark Eleven, who I had just signed. It was Michael Ryan from The Bodines' new band, and I had popped in to hear a new song he had written. I remember somebody was chugging away on a guitar really, really loudly in another room and you could hear it through all the other rehearsal room walls. It was sort of like T. Rex, but it wasn't quite T. Rex, but it was a boogie and that must have been Noel, and it went on for hours.

I now realise that I ran into Noel a couple of other times before that as well, but hadn't known who he was. I think I briefly met him at Reading Festival in 1989. It was backstage when New Order, Sugarcubes and The House of Love were playing. He must have been about twenty-two and had just started roadying with Inspiral Carpets. I was with Debbie and The House of Love had just played. Noel was there because the Inspirals were playing. He was going out with a young member of my staff at Creation, Hannah, and she introduced us. I had no idea who he was, but he would have known who I was because she had told him all the stories about Creation and just how insane it was. I think they went out for about three months. I shook hands with Noel, and then five years later, when I met him again, he changed my life. At that time Noel was the super roadie. Like Davo, who worked with Mick Jones and The Stone Roses: the rock star roadie. Noel was always the coolest guy on the stage, whether he was in the band or not, and the girls always loved him. I think that's what Noel was – the cool guy in the Inspirals camp who ended up being the biggest rock star in the country, like it was his destiny! Every Manchester band had a cool guy in the camp at that time, either on stage or usually as the drug dealer. It was the one with the best clothes who wasn't really in the band, but kind of in the band.

After the Glasgow gig and before we signed them we had a few nights out proper, when Noel would come down to London and hang out for the weekend and go to Andy Weatherall's Sabresonic night. He was really into that freaky end-of-the-house scene, which people don't expect. I guess when you get big the edges get smoothed out. People think they know you but they only know a narrow version of you. He's making sophisticated pop music now with his solo stuff, but he's pretty rough and cool and a really multi-faceted character deep down. I remember when I first met him he was still upset that he had got the sack from the Inspirals. He told me this amazing thing – if there are five floors to the music business, then he'd already been on the third floor with Clint and Inspiral Carpets who were big at the time but he was going up to the fifth floor. He had soaked up the knowledge and he knew his destiny. He also had the songs, and had learned from what he had seen touring the world with the Inspirals. He is perhaps the smartest person I've ever met in a band. He knew exactly what he was doing. His choice of record label was correct. His choice of manager was correct, and getting the management right is really hard. I don't think Noel ever took me seriously, to be absolutely honest. I don't know if he takes that many people seriously. I think he just thinks that this works for him, whatever it is, so that's cool. He may have been more into the idea of me and Creation, but whatever it was it really fucking worked.

Signing Oasis was so random. I remember just after we had signed the band we were making the promotional plan. We thought maybe two years to get out there. A two-year plan to try and make it happen. I knew we would pull it off to a certain level but I had no idea how fast it was going to be. I thought that maybe we would get *The Word* – that TV show – that we would maybe get an *NME* record of the week, and maybe get it onto daytime Radio One. I thought there would be some kind of buzz, but it happened so quickly that we'd achieved all our two-year goals by the second single. That was ridiculous and brilliant. For a normal band, if you got that plan to work in two years it would have been amazing, but this was in a couple of months. It was then we realised we had a runaway train. We knew the band was genius and that Noel was totally sussed and Liam was a total rock star, and it was just a matter of how you bring everyone else on board.

From the start, Oasis were ready for the big time. They expected it and were comfy with that kind of thing because they really wanted it. They didn't want to return to being a small cult band. That wasn't part of their thinking. Just after we signed them we used to have these conversations with me, Noel, a couple of people from the label and the Creation speed dealer in the pub. Noel would say they were going to be the biggest band in the world, and I would humour him and say ok, alright, not because they were not any good but because there were a few hurdles to get over before that happened, but then they just smashed those out of the water. Noel probably wouldn't admit it now, but I think he was probably just talking the talk and then it actually happened. And it was like, fuck! I think 100 per cent that it was a self-fulfilling prophecy.

The point where it started to happen was really early on with the reactions to 'Columbia', which we released just after we signed them in 1993. When we pushed that out as a white label to music writers, which was what we did with new bands, a few of them thought it was pretty special. There was this hub of people who could see it happening – me, Johnny Hopkins, who was head of press for Creation at the time, and music writers like Paul Mathur at *Melody Maker*, Andrew Perry and John Robb. Also the label and the band just knew. We believed it. And somehow, it fucking started to smoulder and then, when it really caught fire, we were playing fucking catch-up. I was surprised, of course, but then how many times have we set records up and it doesn't happen?

The important thing for a label is to get that raw talent and make sure it's recorded and presented properly. We had a vision and Noel had a vision and we made it work. The other key thing for a label is having the team and the contacts to get it out there, and then being crazy enough to believe that it could actually really work. Ironically, nobody at the record company was ever really that interested in finding a new band, but when Oasis happened then every fucker claimed that they had helped me find them! Thank god Oasis were always fucking cool about it. They always said that 'It was McGee that found us'.

Within a few records, Oasis were bigger than we could ever have dreamed, but could they go supernova? It took a pop culture moment for Oasis to truly break big. Pop culture is driven by fads and fashions. I was caught up in some of them, like glam, punk and acid house, but they were the good ones. Those created by the media and the music biz are never the same as the ones that come from the street. When you run a label, though, you have to be aware of what's going on, and if it works to your advantage then great, but you must always be aware of your own pop art aesthetic as well. Britpop was the moment, but it was just a fucking marketing term. I thought it was rubbish even though I sold a lot of records because of it. At the time, it was used as a marketing term, with all these stores selling records in truckloads. I remember one day Oasis shipped 50,000 records to HMV as part of the store's Britpop promotion, and their manager Marcus Russell insisted that we took them all back out of the shops because they didn't want to be part of it. Oasis would also pull out of a big Britpop TV special that Damon Albarn was hosting because they didn't see themselves as part of that scene. For them, it was too short term and someone else's creation. Oasis saw themselves as a classic rock 'n' roll band and not as a Britpop band.

I hated Britpop. People might think that makes me a hypocrite but I don't care. Oasis would have made it anyway and were not part of all that, and Creation was already Creation. I thought Britpop was bollocks, though it was good for the label and very good to me.

Oasis was starting to take off anyway, despite Britpop, and then they got their big break when Damon created the whole Oasis v Blur chart battle, when he deliberately moved the release of Blur's August 1995 single, 'Country House', the first from their *The Great Escape* album, to clash with the release of Oasis's 'Roll With It' single.

In a way, I may have had a hand in it as well. Before the big chart battle, the initial skirmishes had been at the Brit Awards earlier that year. Blur won the Best Band award and Oasis were the Best Newcomer. Noel and Liam were heckling Blur all through the ceremony. Oddly, though, I was mates with Blur. I already knew them from around town, but didn't register the brewing rivalry until I threw a party in May 1995 to celebrate Oasis's first number 1 with 'Some Might Say'. The rivalry that had been simmering since spring 1994, when 'Supersonic' came out at the same time as Blur's *Parklife* album was going to go supernova. Because I'd been friends with Damon Albarn for some time, I invited him to the party. Of course, Noel and Liam were pissed off when they heard that Blur were coming, and I must admit I liked the idea that it was causing a bit of friction. That's part of running a label – sometimes you just have to tear the narrative a little bit. Create a situation. See what happens. For Blur, the rivalry was all a bit of a laugh – they didn't seem to realise how serious Oasis were about it all. It was a jape for Blur, but for the brothers from a council estate in Burnage, being in a band was the real deal. Liam, being Liam, spent the evening relentlessly taking the piss out of Damon. He kept going at him about being number 1 in a deliberately childish way. Obviously, Damon being Damon left the party planning on getting his own back and, along with his label boss and band mentor, the late Andy Ross, they decided to get the next Blur single to go up against us. What had started as a laugh for one band was fast turning into something else.

Both bands were about to release albums – Blur with *The Great Escape* and Oasis with *(What's The Story) Morning Glory?* – Britpop was breaking big, and Blur were the golden boys of the scene. Both bands had singles due in August – Oasis had 'Roll With It' on 14 August and Blur had 'Country House' out the week after, but things were about to change. The fallout from the party had triggered something in Damon, who decided to move his single to the same week to compete with Oasis in a head-to-head for the number 1 spot. Damon was very competitive in those days and the battle that defined Britpop was about to start.

Oasis were behind Blur at that point by quite a long way. Blur were the main band, but that chart battle brought us into the ring and then it was like The Beatles v the Stones. We went from being big to supernova. We were all over the daily papers and TV news. Every label needs a big break and they don't come much bigger than that. Suddenly we were getting major coverage.

It was like the battle for the soul of British pop culture split neatly along north v south, middle v working class, art school v council estate. It was such a great story and was a gift to Oasis and Creation because it put us in the middle of not just Britpop or pop culture but the proper news. Our small indie label and the working-class Burnage boys were getting the kind of exposure that we could only have dreamt of. There was no stopping us now, and Oasis were on the way to becoming the biggest band in the world, thanks to Damon.

Initially, Blur won the first round and got the number 1 single because they were on a major. Even if I was a bit dubious about the chart battle at first because I thought we would get battered and even if we had lost the first round it was going to go through the roof. It was Oasis's management at Ignition who were really up for it, and they were right in the end. I must admit it was a great pop culture moment but we never took it that seriously. The Blur camp seemed much more competitive than ours, and if we lost the first round we won the more important album second round by a knockout!

Blur and the EMI juggernaut had got the number 1 single and their champagne moment. I knew Creation couldn't compete. We were an independent and Blur had the might of EMI behind them with all of their marketing tricks. Plus we had problems with the barcode that wouldn't register. But whilst they may have won the first battle, they lost the war because Oasis had the tunes, so when it came to the albums it was a different story. If Damon thought his victory would shut down the taunts from Oasis then he was wrong. Very wrong. When our album came out it went ballistic. We sold 350,000 copies in the first week. The people had spoken! Oasis would go on to sell more than 20 million copies of that album worldwide, which was far more than Blur or all of Britpop put together.

Even without the chart battle I still think Oasis would have been a big band. It was just a case of how big. They would have ended up as a festival headliner kind of big band, but the chart battle took us to another level. We went from being on the outside into the full public glare and the public liked what they saw. It showed that as a record label you have to be ready for anything and see what works for your bands.

For me, it was a great opportunity, and also full of great pop culture fun and mischief, but Oasis, being Oasis, took the whole thing much more seriously than I did and decided to hate Blur. And Blur, being Blur, thought it was a bit of a laugh and that made things worse. They were really rubbing each other up the wrong way. The story itself was kinda perfect in that the two bands were seen as representing the two ends of British pop culture. It became a sort of class war as well. Damon was seen as a middle-class kid trying to be working class, and that wound Oasis up.

It was the same with their management. I loved Andy Ross – Blur's manager at the time – but during an 'in conversation' we both did in 2018, he still seemed to be fighting the Britpop battles. It was like he was still in that moment. I was sat there thinking, 'Andy, did you not get the memo? it was all showbiz!' For me, it was just a bit of fun, and it really doesn't matter anymore. Andy was talking about this band he was looking after at the time called Diesel Park West and how they thought Oasis were rubbish. I was sat there thinking, who the fuck are Diesel Park West? I still don't know who the fuck they are. Well, maybe a little bit... As the conversation continued, it seemed to me that he was still charging like the light brigade at the front line of that pop war, led by Diesel Park West, who were actually his priority band, whilst Blur were almost like an accident!

It gets like that when you run a label. You get obsessed with one of your bands. You can't understand why no one else gets them. You have to be careful to not take your eye off the ball and miss the main chance. Maybe it was the same thing with me and Primal Scream – they were always my band and I always worked hard to get them to make it, but all the other bands kept blowing up instead. In the end, we hit the right formula with Primal Scream and they became one of our main bands. They did what every great band does by synthesising the moment. They captured acid house but made something else out of it – this was so much more interesting than the retro knees-up of Britpop when it arrived.

Of course, as a record label, we were also pragmatic. We were not fools and though we might have hated the term Britpop, one of the key things in running a record label is taking an opportunity if it's right in front of you. So when Britpop became a scene in 1994, we were not shy of pushing a few of our bands in that direction. It certainly didn't harm the prospects of The Boo Radleys, who had started out a more left-field proposition with *Giant Steps*, but in March 1995 their follow-up album *Wake Up* was much more of the moment and a massive smash, driven by the 'Wake Up Boo' single, which was all over the radio and a massive hit. It sent the album to number 1 and the band were suddenly and unexpectedly in the mainstream world. As soon as they had that success they went all cool and indie, and went back to their weird indie music press records that no one was interested in.

To this day Oasis still feel like an archetypal Creation band, despite their success dwarfing both the label and the indie scene. If there was ever a label and a band perfectly suited to each other, then this was it. Of course, it was already there in the few songs they played that night at King Tut's in Glasgow when I chanced on them, and I knew there was much more. But the Britpop thing upped the stakes, and when that starts it's sort of an unstoppable thing. And everyone wants a bit of it.

CHAPTER 12

....

Stick with your vision and trust your instinct

I had done my research, buying all those singles as a kid. Whether it was Bowie, Sweet, Jethro Tull or Mungo Jerry, I listened to everything. I looked at the sleeves. I wondered about the producers, and the record labels that released them. And when I started reading the music press I became as obsessed by the people who shaped these musical visions, like Malcolm McLaren, Seymour Stein, Tony Wilson and Andrew Loog Oldham. These people were visionaries who did things on their own terms. They are the real heroes for me.

In my head, I'm still a ginger punk rocker from Glasgow, and that's what I'm always going to be. I've never had a particularly high opinion of myself, and being old is irrelevant because I'm still into music. My role models are those managers, and Seymour more than anyone else. He was still running around in music at the age of eighty. That's how I want to be: still into bands and still putting music out, right to the very end. Initially, when Creation started, I was living out my fantasy of being one of these people. In the end, I certainly sold more records than Malcolm, but I was culturally much less important than him. These people totally changed the scene. They thought of pop culture in the big 360. They understood it all. I was just a music nut releasing music I instinctively loved.

Even though the music was the main force, and the culture another big part, the main drive of Creation was to make money out of music and escape having to have a shitty job and a shitty life – that used to be the driving force of rock 'n' roll, didn't it? The escape from drudgery. It was the working-class dream. Yet even though that was crucial, it still had to be on my own terms. That's not to say I would have done anything to achieve that aim. There was a kind of music that I was obsessed with. I had a vision, and I had to make some money out of it.

In business terms, Creation started as one thing and by the mid-nineties had morphed into another. We started as the little guys, but after Oasis we were in the mainstream and that was what we'd always wanted. We had gone from being a bedroom DIY label to being a big business. A large part of the vision was to take the music, and our take on pop art, into the mainstream. To take the 'magnificent failures' in art and music that had so thrilled Malcolm McLaren, and then place them in the mainstream as he had done with the Sex Pistols. I may have liked a lot of underground music at the time – like post-punk bands, The Velvet Underground, and many of the groups that I had been putting on at The Living Room – but I didn't want it to stay in the underground. I wanted our culture in the mainstream. I was inspired by The Jam in the late seventies, who not only wrote great songs that really connected with people like me, but also took pop art into the real world. They were one of those classic bands, like The Smiths, The Stone Roses, Oasis and Arctic Monkeys, that united British youth. We could identify with Paul Weller because he was just like us. Not only could you see yourself in Paul but he also wrote songs that could touch everyone. The Jam had taken these pop art and pop culture ideas to number 1 and showed us that pop could be more than just great songs. They were an exciting band with exciting ideas and great songs, and the biggest band in the UK after punk.

That's the kind of thing I wanted and a crucial part of the vision of running my own record label. No one else on the post-punk scene seemed to want that. Or if they did they were not admitting it. In that world, it was thought to be cool to stay underground and play music to your mates or the people that 'understood' it. I was working class and from Glasgow and much more populist. A rock 'n' roll populist.

Indie itself is a much misunderstood word. These days it's a handy section in a high-street record store, but in the post-punk period it was an ideological standpoint. It had been done before but not as seamlessly as this. My idea of what pop culture – and by extension a record label – could be was different from everyone else's, and that clarity is key to running a label. An indie label is far more of an art concept than a business. And a true indie label is like a true indie band – it's a vision thing. The big labels may be into the art of business, but the pure heart of indies was always more about the business of art. A maverick label like Creation could only exist if it was true to its vision. And when it comes to realising the vision, I've always lived on instinct. Go with your gut. It's the only path. Don't listen to people when they tell you to stop. I still go off a gut instinct. If I like it and feel it, I sign it. That's true of every band I have ever signed. It's always been that way. Whether it was going down the David Bowie rabbit hole as a kid, or signing Oasis on that famous night in Glasgow when no one else gave a fuck about them, I trust my gut. Then I go gung ho. Once I decide I'm totally in there, there are no half-measures.

So many people work in the music industry as though it's a career option. Which is what it has become – a respectable job in the entertainment industry. Good for a mortgage, terrible for art. That's not right for me, because, of all the businesses in the world, this is the one that thrives on the mavericks and risk-takers. Most great records were made by people prepared to take a chance and trust their instinct and it's the same with the labels. Initially, the Creation releases were like experiments seeking a high-decibel alchemy. The Mary Chain were the first perfectly realised version and Oasis the maximum. The wall-of-sound guitars with a psychedelic twist was always somewhere near the Creation main deck. To this day, Oasis may have been the 'biggest band in the world', but they still feel very much like a Creation archetype.

Creation may have ended up with its own house style, but we took many risks to get there. Every step of the way it was a mixture of blind faith, wild certainty, bravado, and a deep belief in my instinct. Whereas most people would see a band and fall in love with their indefinable thing, and then persuade themselves why they should not put that band out in a battle between the conscious and subconscious minds, I was the opposite. I would fall in love with a band's music or attitude, or the characters in the group, and then try and get them to make it. I liked those wild-eyed ideas machine musicians who would demand the impossible and walk the talk; for me, those are the characters who are always going to make it. Whether they sell out stadiums or become shadowy cult figures, they still have something. Something magnetic. Something wild. Something melodic. A hook.

Music is all about instinct. You just *know*. It's like a lightbulb going off in your head. I knew the records I loved as a kid as soon as the needle hit the groove. Pop culture is a fast culture. You don't need to analyse it. You just know. Sometimes I would get it totally wrong, with people like Momus or The Jazz Butcher, who made genius records but didn't sell as many as Oasis, but that wasn't the point. I've never signed people because I thought they could sell, I sign people because I think they're good and then try and get them to connect with people. I sign people because I believe in them and I want to work with them. It's total instinct. It might be nutty but I rely on it. I trust it. Ultimately, though, it's always about the song – and you instantly know that when you hear it. When you get the character *and* the song, then you have the moment.

Succeeding in the rock 'n' roll business is half instinct and half luck. It's an indefinable kind of thing – often I think, how come no one else can see this? Even if everyone was looking the other way, that wouldn't stop me from getting involved. I was not interested in what other people thought. Maybe in the early days of Creation, this was easier and it was purer because the choices were not commercial because there was no hope of the bands being commercial. I would only make decisions for the art, like bringing in Andy Weatherall to work with Primal Scream, and those decisions ironically ended up being more commercial.

It was like when I first met Noel Gallagher. I didn't have a clue that Oasis could be big. I just thought they were a great band and so I signed them, and as it grew I realised that this could be really big. Initially, though, I had no idea that they were going to sell as many as they did. I liked the band, and Noel was one of those characters. I knew straight away that he had something nobody else had. I could just feel it. Everyone else had passed on him but I knew straight away that he was great, and so was his band. Most of the characters I signed had no idea what they had, but Noel was the only person I met that knew what and where the goal was, and how he was going to get there and score, and that was impressive. With Primal Scream and their key members, Bobby, Innes and Robert, they might have known where the goal was but they tended to forget about two or three lines in. Literally.

This vision thing is fundamental to running an indie label and you must always stay true to your ideas – you can take mad tangents and wild U-turns like I did when I got really into acid house, but the main core of your ideal should still be there. Many people in the music business are careful and try to replicate formulae and stay where the money is and with what is selling, and that's understandable. Even I did that now and then, maybe with indie guitar bands, but for me it was about the moments when I got transfixed and spellbound. That moment of conversion. Of instinct. Like when I started releasing dance records or signed maverick bands like Five Go Down To The Sea? when the label started. It was all part of my vision at those given times. I just wanted everyone else to understand what I felt. That's why I signed the bands and released the music.

For every Noel Gallagher signed after a drunken night in Glasgow, there were countless Five Go Down To The Sea? type bands signed to the label, which were built around other wild characters who had sparked my instinct and made genius records that were roundly ignored, but they are equally important in the Creation story. It wasn't always the making it. It was often the recognising of it. Never trust a hippy, but always trust your instinct.

CHAPTER 13

....

Dealing with
egos and superstars

My teenage years playing in bands gave me a
real insight into how bands work and how
the relationships between band members and
managers work. It also meant that bands trusted me. They
knew that I knew about the dynamics of being in a band and
what being in a band felt like. I understood what they hoped
for, the dreams and the graft, and how difficult it is to be in
a band. I understood that weird language of being in a band.
Even a bedroom band. This was key to communicating with
musicians at the record label.

Loads of bands don't get on with each other. That's just the normal state of things. I try and fix that by speaking to them and understanding the dynamics of their band. It's a key part of what I do, both when I was at Creation and now as a manager. The problem with music is that we are all fucking mad. Maybe me being as mad as – or madder than – the bands helped, because I'm good at working with these kinds of characters. Bands fascinate me. They also help me make sense of myself and my life. I'm similar to them. The only difference is that I own the label and know how it all works, and they have the guitars and the songs. Someone once described my bands as weirdos who love a melody, and that's fine by me. Perfect, in fact. All the best music is made by misfits and outsiders and I just have to look after them and guide them towards the mainstream and help them survive.

We also had this space at Creation that was mental, especially once Tim Abbot got on board in 1991 and helped me run the label. Creation after acid house was a non-stop party. This was living the dream. In some ways, Creation itself was like a band. We lived it large and we lived it fast. We were going the same speed as the bands. Sometimes faster. The people that ran the label were also in bands and it gave the label the same rock 'n' roll dynamic. We were living the life of drugs, swimming pools and girls that we had read about in books. But we also managed to get the records out and set the bands up properly. Somehow we made cash from chaos and there was a method in the madness. What band wouldn't thrive in an atmosphere like that? That's how to run a record label.

In both management and with a label, it's important to look after that collective state of mind. To look after each other. Running a record label is like a football manager running a changing room, with a mixture of small bands, hopeful new bands and superstars. And they don't come any bigger than Oasis and the Gallaghers. That period was like being Alex Ferguson on steroids. Maybe for Oasis I was like a music biz version of a dysfunctional surrogate father in the early days – it can get like that sometimes with bands – but then I was crazier than they were at the time, so perhaps not.

Working with Oasis was always genius, wild and unpredictable. You never knew where you were with them. They were so volatile, but I loved it. The Gallaghers had such different personalities.

I loved Noel from day one. He was a genius hustler and he hustled me into doing the deal! The first time he came down the stairs into the Creation office, he clocked the posters of Lowell George, George Harrison and Paul Simonon on the walls, and when I sat down with him I asked him what music he liked, and he said 'Music made by people like George Harrison, Lowell George and Paul Simonon,' and I thought, fucking great, he is one of ours. He had already played me! He was one of the gang and I just thought he was mental like me and that we had the same taste.

Oasis were everything I had always dreamt of releasing with Creation. They were rock 'n' roll, they had a psychedelic edge, but it was tougher and more working class, and they had those anthems. They also had Noel and Liam, who were about to be the two most famous people of the decade. They had the charisma and the whiff of danger, especially when they were together, which was pure excitement. Even their interviews were explosive. You just didn't know what was going to happen next. They would be at each other's throats, like in the 1994 John Harris *NME* interview that was so funny and cool that it was later released as a vinyl album. In the interview, Noel and Liam were arguing over the band being deported before they had got to Holland to play their first European gig. There had been a drunken kick-off on the boat that Noel had not taken part in, and in the interview he was still annoyed and wanted the band's music to be taken seriously, whereas Liam was all about rock 'n' roll and they ended up having this four-letter slanging match. Fierce Panda Records decided to release the recording as a single by splitting the interview in half and releasing it as 'Wibbling Rivalry' in 1995, which charted at number 52 on the UK chart, making it the most commercially successful interview release of all time. Oasis were so big that even their interviews were hits.

They were the perfect band for that moment. It was the first time in a long time that rock 'n' roll felt this dangerous. It has now become very boring and safe and people now do interviews in PR speak, but Noel and Liam were off the cuff. They said it as they felt it and that connected with millions of people. They were also fearless, and that's why I loved them.

Oasis at their peak were in the rarefied zone of superstardom that few bands reach. Their sales figures were ridiculously high and their gigs were major events. The band had gone beyond the big league and into that rare space of bands like The Beatles, the Stones and Led Zep – total rock classics. Watching Oasis in their pomp was like watching a band that you knew trampling around in that fabled world that you had only read about in Beatles books.

Every time I met them, something crazy would happen, even if it was at someone else's event, and I loved that. I had signed Idha, Andy Bell from Ride's wife, to Creation, and was having a showcase for her at Ronnie Scott's in Soho. I'd hired Sean O'Hagan to work on the project and do the strings on the album as well as live, and it probably cost me 100 grand to make the record. Idha is quite a vulnerable person and I thought that at any minute she would walk out with nerves. So we were being very, very protective of her. Alex Lowe, who had a new band with Andy Bell called Hurricane #1, was at the gig. He had just done this interview in the *NME* where he had said 'these cunts, Oasis', which he didn't mean – that's just the way we talk in Glasgow. That's affectionate! Of course, I knew what he meant, but Liam had taken it upon himself to front out Alex. So Liam turns up at the showcase and he's in a mood. Despite Oasis being literally the biggest band in the world, he's decided to sort this out. Personally.

He goes over to Alex at the gig and punches him. I'm thinking, bad move, because Alex is a boxer and can actually fucking fight properly. But Liam's got a big West Ham football hooligan security guy – a fucking terrier. I think he was like six foot six and hovering in the background. Anyway, Liam and Alex start tussling and it becomes very apparent that Alex is utterly capable and getting the upper hand. Alex had Liam in the corner against the wall and Liam's bouncer is moving over. Meanwhile, Alex is dancing like a boxer and hitting Liam and it's not going well, and somehow this goes on for ten minutes and the crowd are leaving the building. What Liam hadn't banked on was that Alex is insane and doesn't back down. The only person in the room that could get Alex to calm down was the man that owned Alex's and Liam's record contract – me. So I tell Alex to calm down, whilst Liam is screaming abuse at me. I have no idea how it had all become my fault. Maybe because I had stopped the fight. So

I manage to get them outside, and there's a famous picture of me and Liam outside Ronnie Scott's where it looks like we are having a chat, but what he's really saying is 'McGee's a fucking cunt!' to my face. We then went to some drinking club, some posh place like upstairs at the Groucho, and we were in the very back and Liam shouts at me for two hours. It's like the blast furnace treatment until he eventually runs out of steam. It was nuts.

The next day I'm supposed to go for a meeting with Marcus Russell – the Oasis manager – and Liam, and I'm dreading it as I was in recovery at the time from my own drink and drug demons and pretty fragile, and trying to keep away from drinking situations and to avoid full-on aggressive arguments with people because it was just not good for me. So I go into this meeting and Liam gets up and hugs me and it totally took me by surprise because I was expecting round two but it wasn't that at all. It was lovely. And he asks if I want to meet the Dalai Lama. And I was like, no. Are you scared? he asked. I said I wasn't scared, even though I now had a fear of flying after my breakdown on the plane a couple of years before. Now I couldn't get on a plane because it was too claustrophobic for me after I'd had a druggy meltdown on a flight to LA. Liam said, 'You're fucking scared.' Of course, being from Glasgow, I couldn't back down and I said, 'Ok I'll go!' So I got it arranged with the Dalai Lama's people that me and Liam Gallagher are going to fly to Nepal and go up the hill and meet him. Oasis were the biggest band in the world and they can get a meeting like this. They had met Yoko Ono and Bowie, and they were flying at that level where they got to meet everybody. So it was all arranged, and a few weeks later Liam goes, 'If we go there will be none of that John Lennon/Brian Epstein shit,' referencing the rumour about Lennon and Epstein having an affair on a holiday just before Beatlemania. I was not that bothered by it because so many people accuse me of being gay that I just ignore it.

So I think, I'm going to Nepal, so I better get a malaria jab. What nobody knew at the time was that malaria jabs can sometimes send people crazy. They can be pretty horrible and people get really ill because of the side-effects, but I'm just about to go and get my fucking malaria shot when Liam phones up. 'It's Liam – we're not going to Nepal. I can't go, Patsy won't let me...'

And that was that, but also very much a Liam tale and an example of how it was working with Oasis at the time, and all the different sides and facets to Liam. There's a lot of depth to him – one minute he's brawling, and the next he's wanting to meet the Dalai Lama. It's a depth that people don't see, wrapped in a toughness, like when he came back after Oasis had split and after Beady Eye had ended, and made a solo career for himself, which is so hard to do.

By the end of 1996, Oasis were peak superstar. No band had got this big in the UK for decades. We had sold millions of records and were flying. We were in completely new territory and dealing with it as we went along. The success was amazing, of course, but that level of fame brings its own pressures. It was time for the third Oasis album. The band certainly had a work ethic. So they started recording at Abbey Road – where else? Liam got busted for coke and got a caution, and it was all going crazy. It was right at the peak of that cocaine on cornflakes period, which was a mad time when Oasis were living the rock 'n' roll lifestyle to the hilt and being totally open about it in the media, with Noel comparing taking cocaine to drinking tea and famously saying that he sprinkled it on his cornflakes every day.

The coke and the madness was an influence on how 1997's *Be Here Now* album sounded. It was the band's superstar album. So of course it was big and overblown and everything was loud. There was layer after layer of guitars and it was in your face and bombastic. In hindsight, people see *Be Here Now* as the point when it all started to go wrong for Oasis, but I still believe in that album. There are great songs on there, it's just the production that lets it down. Noel always said this was the coke album and it showed. There was way too much coke in the studio and that made the album sonically different because of the way that coke affects your hearing;

it was all top-end and no bottom-end. Added to this, the producer, Owen Morris, had been getting burned and had lost the plot. He was as off it as the band were. I went down to the studio at Ridge Farm and it was coke and loud guitars and overdubs everywhere. Also, some of the songs were long. Very long. Very coked-up long.

Hindsight is a wonderful thing when you are running a record label, but not that useful at the time. The album was too overblown, and had maybe lost that street charm that made the band so loved. The whole campaign for the album only added to this. It wasn't the way I would have done it. Things had got too big and too messy. The band's management were running the show and had an embargo on the review copies of the album being sent out to journalists, and that managed to piss off all the media, with everyone having to sign a non-disclosure agreement to review it. Crazy. It really pissed people off and, because our name was on the agreement, people thought it was our doing and it left a bad taste in people's mouths and meant they had it in for the band and the label. Things were changing in music and these sorts of agreements were becoming out of date. With the internet now starting to make serious inroads, it was becoming impossible to stop leaks of new albums. This heavy-handed media approach played against Oasis, who had been seen as a people's band. They were like your mates in the pub, not some remote corporate entity bullying their way around. They were punk rock in that kind of way. They may have sold millions of records but they still felt like they belonged to the people. The *Be Here Now* campaign only served to alienate them from their fans and supporters.

Whilst all this was going on, their support band nicked in and made the album of the year – The Verve's *Urban Hymns* was massive, and though Oasis still sold 11 million copies of *Be Here Now*, it felt like a failure. It was the end of an era and the album was seen as a marker of the end of Britpop. The huge success of the band, and the other bands that were a part of that scene, make it one of the biggest music movements ever produced in the UK, but that same success was also part of its failure. By 1997 the other bands were moving on and changing their music and the scene that had thrived on adversity, on its outsider nature, was over because it was now the mainstream. There is always a hangover after the mad days of music scenes – whether it's punk or acid house – and it was the same with Britpop. Things were burning out and falling apart. Primal Scream released *Vanishing Point* and it was a dark yet ambitious record and remarkably hit number 2 in the charts and sold 300,000 albums. I loved it, but it was like the comedown record. Its darkness is its genius. Once it would have been a major victory that an album so daring could have done that well, but in the post-Britpop years of 1997 onwards, it felt like a failure because it was a comedown from the millions that we had been selling a couple of years before. That was how mad it had all got – it was bonkers to think that just because you couldn't sell groundbreaking albums in vast quantities anymore, you were failing. In reality, getting to number 2 with such a non-commercial album was a major victory.

Coping with Oasis was an object lesson in how to run an indie label. But after Oasis things started going back to normal, returning to the mundane, and I was starting to drift.

PART THREE

The Comedown and Rebirth

CHAPTER 14

....

Drugs

Drugs are intrinsic to music culture. Every new wave of drugs changed pop culture dramatically – from the mods and speed to the hippies and LSD, from the punks' return to speed, from the cocaine-fuelled eighties to the E-driven acid house explosion to the mess heroin made of people's lives. By the nineties, there was a smorgasbord of dangerous delights to be had at Creation; when it came to the drugs train, we were more gung ho than any other record label. It was amazing that anything got done, but with a weird mixture of a protestant work ethic and maybe a protestant partying ethic, the label not only survived but thrived. The upside, apart from the good times, was being in touch with a scene that was full of drugs. For Creation, it was, quite literally, a high point, and we made sense of it with some astonishing releases and a reckless business plan that created a booming period. As ever, this was not the conventional way to run a record label, but it was a creative period that helped to define the label and forge the prevalent music scene of the moment.

When we started we were not really into drugs. I think the drug phase in my life was maybe caused by Primal Scream However, I'm not blaming them! I think that way of life got inside my head and I thought that's what you were supposed to do. That it was rock 'n' roll. I'm not blaming them because you make your own choices, but I think I normalised it by hanging out with a bunch of fucking nut jobs! Ok, maybe not nut jobs but a bunch of people that fucking got on it all the time!

Also, in 1987 I had split from my first wife, Yvonne, and acid house had started and I got really into that. It was a turning point in my life in many ways. The label was now in the Hackney office, which was a totally different area than it is now. There was nothing around. It was derelict. No neighbours to complain about the noise. Perfect for Interzone all-night parties. It was a wild time and I was the self-medicating doctor who wrote myself a prescription of ecstasy, speed, acid, coke or Jack Daniel's every day. It was not conventional medicine. I also spent a lot of time in

Manchester, where I had more endless parties from 1989 to 1995. Manchester was the perfect place to be at the time if you wanted that kind of lifestyle. I loved the Happy Mondays and I loved ecstasy, and the Happy Mondays had loads of ecstasy. It was a great arrangement and worked for me at a time when it felt like the whole of Manchester was off its collective head. I believe you have to live the life to run a maverick record label, and the music business was a more lawless place in those days.

After acid house, I hung out with Oasis, which was exhausting. They were non-stop on coke and so was I. I just never stopped. I would go from one night with Liam and Noel recording the album in Wales, to spending a few nights out with Primal Scream – and you can imagine what that was like. Different people and more drugs. I didn't realise that the bands dipped in and out of it and that I was the only one who never had a night off. I was on it 24/7. It had become my normal life.

When success came, I was trying to deal with my drug problem. It was starting to seriously affect me. I remember when I was given the Godlike Genius award by the *NME* in 1996 and I was too mashed to go and get it. By then the real madness was beginning to creep in. Every label should have a chance to go there! They were strange times and strange things were happening. I was doing mad stuff. I bought a full page in the *NME* to print a letter about how brilliant the reformed Sex Pistols gig was; I bought Noel a chocolate-brown Rolls-Royce and a watch for Liam that cost over ten grand. Those were the cocaine years, when I would be caning it with Noel and Liam, going crazy with Bobby or Throb, getting smashed in the office or raving in a club. It was non-stop and I was still running a record label. I would be in a club all night and when it came time to get to the airport to go to a meeting in LA, I would grab a cab and get down to Heathrow. Because I was still bouncing, I would neck a valium to try and get some sleep, and then get off the plane in LA rough as fuck and head straight off to the next party. The days and nights and continents all blurred into one.

The final night of this lifestyle came in 1994 when I was sitting on a plane going to LA in the middle of a several-days-long drink and drugs binge. I left a party at Primal Scream's rehearsal room in Waterloo on top of a two-day bender with Oasis, who were not just burning the candle at both ends but incinerating it. They had the debut album in the bag and just knew they were going to be massive and were celebrating before the event. To excess. And of course, I had to accompany my bands all the time and keep up with them. That was my duty. So I went from Oasis to the Primals, and I had an added dose of flu which would have sent a normal person to their bed but, you know, duty calls.

DRUGS

As I was leaving the Primals' party and before I got the cab to the airport, Throb rolled out a huge line of coke which I snorted. It would have been rude not to. Now I was ready for LA. I was running the world's most hedonistic party label. If pop culture was a hurricane we were right at the epicentre. Or maybe we were the hurricane. My instinct always drew me to the heart of the culture, whether it was the music or the lifestyle. That's important in rock 'n' roll and it was how to run a record label. Or so I thought. The problem is, you can't run a label like that for ever. Or maybe you can, but you certainly cannot run your body like that.

I met my sister Susan, who was coming with me on this trip, and we got in a taxi to rush to Heathrow to get the plane to LA to continue the party. It was her first trip there and we were going to hang out and have a good time with my rock 'n' roll friends. However, that one massive line of coke before I left the party had sent me over the edge and my heart was pounding like crazy and I could hear voices inside my head. I didn't feel good and I knew I needed to come down. Or calm down. I remembered that I normally carried Valium or Temazepam on me, so I frantically patted my jacket, looking for them, but I'd forgotten my pills. It totally freaked me out, and when I was on the plane I had some sort of breakdown. I was not in a good place, so the air hostesses phoned ahead for an ambulance for when we landed. When I got off the plane I knew I was in deep trouble as I was surrounded by the guys in orange jumpsuits. The medics. The serious crew. They were running round me doing all the checks. They measured my blood pressure and it was not looking good. They were muttering that my life was at risk. They said I had nervous exhaustion, which means straight to rehab, do not pass go. They were looking pretty worried and that didn't make me feel any better. They thought I might be having a heart attack. They were worried that I was going to die.

The thing is, I was in such a mad state that, even when they had calmed me down and sorted me out, I just went back to the hotel and forgot about the incident straight away. I brushed it aside as a one-off, and then it was time to get down to more serious duties. I needed to show my sister a good time in LA. So I just kept caning it, as we went to see Swervedriver at the Whisky a Go Go. I felt I was invincible and that it was totally normal to live your life at this speed, so I did a bottle of whisky and guzzled some pills.

Somehow, the next day I went for a meeting at Warners but my mind was all over the place and I felt like I was tripping and only just got through it. Back at the Mondrian Hotel, my body was going into hypertension. I was actually Totally Wired, like Mark E Smith had once sung in The Fall. I thought I was having a heart attack and crawled down to reception and they called an ambulance. Again they turned up in their orange jumpsuits and carried me out and it finally registered that I was in the shit. The deep shit.

I spent two weeks flat out in the hospital with wires coming out of me. My body had shut down. I was in a mess. Eventually, I managed to crawl out to see The Jesus And Mary Chain record a video with Hope Sandoval. Jim Reid took one look at me and mumbled sardonically, 'I thought you were dead.' I had to get Ed Ball to fly from Japan, where he was playing keyboards with The Boo Radleys, to LA and fly home with me. I was a wreck and couldn't face being on a plane on my own. Then I went into rehab at the Charter Nightingale in Lisson Grove, which obviously made running a record label a bit difficult for some time.

I had been partying non-stop for six or seven years and I was burned out. My guess is that it all got out of control because we were all normal people and not hardened drug takers. In the end a few of us burned out, but we were the lucky ones. We drank and did drugs and then we fell off the horse because, unlike the late Throb, we could not take it. What he was into was not really normal; for him it was the lifestyle of thirty years, from the early days of Primal Scream, that did him in. He was never a junkie though, just a lifestyle drug user. I couldn't keep up with that level, though, and that's what burned me out. So here was the boss of Creation lying in bed for weeks, itching to get back into the hedonistic saddle of the wildest horse in town and be part of the world that my label had soundtracked and created. I still hadn't learned that you don't have to live that mad lifestyle 24/7. It is a lesson that should be learned by anyone in rock 'n' roll. Learn from Iggy Pop – switch on and off. On stage he's Iggy whilst off stage he's James Osterberg. My mistake was believing that not only was I Iggy, but that I was expected to live out the rock 'n' roll party 24/7.

This sounds mental but I enjoyed my time in rehab. It felt great to calm down. I got myself sober, which was hard work, and after that it was enjoyable. In many ways, I think that on the plane and in LA I had made some kind of breakthrough rather than a breakdown. I realised that I didn't need to play the game the way it was played. I didn't have to be off my head to be rock 'n' roll. I could do this thing and stay sober. I hadn't done anything as mad as my mate Youth from Killing Joke had done years before, when he had been found walking down Tottenham Court Road naked on acid at the end of his first period with the band. Yet he somehow returned to become one of the biggest producers on the planet. So there was a way out.

Of course, I had read about rock 'n' roll burnout but I didn't know it was going to happen to me. My father came down and took me back to Glasgow and I rented a small house out in Renfrew and tried to glue myself back together.

I switched my phone off and tried to block out the insanity of my old world. I sat there watching loads of football and enjoying the silence and learning that I didn't have to run at the speed I had been. I was a millionaire, I could dictate the pace I wanted to go at, and the isolation felt good.

When I came out of rehab in 1994 I went to see Primal Scream play a gig, but they didn't understand what had happened to me. They were too young then. They were full on drugs at that point and they saw rehab as a weakness at the time. Adjusting back to life was not going to be easy. I was certainly not in the right industry for it. The music biz is awash with drugs, and if you are the one who is not taking them you can be treated with suspicion and not be part of the crowd. Just because I had stopped didn't mean that everyone else had stopped. I tried to avoid the drug scene and the people taking drugs, but in the end I had to face it.

Primal Scream persuaded me to come and see them play a gig, which was a benefit for the dockers in Liverpool. I went up there and went in their dressing room for the first time in years. I knew there would be drugs going on, and Bobby necked an E whilst he was talking to me, which made me feel really uncomfortable. I didn't want to be around that kind of thing anymore. For a few years after that, me and Bobby were estranged because of this stuff, and that was difficult because we had grown up together and had been on the trip

– quite literally – since the beginning and were really close friends. But the hedonism had become core to running the record label and that was going to have to change.

Now that I was on the outside of that culture it felt like a totally different world. From now on I would go to the party sober. I was big enough to do that, and my pals understood in the end. Even Primal Scream. I stayed friends with Innes and Bobby and we never talked about it until they had their own addiction issues later on. Bobby became sober in 2008. The thing about it was that it was about sorting yourself out. Oasis understood the way I was even less, but they tried hard and they never gave me a hard time for being sober. I was out of action for about nine months in all, from February 1994, and I hardly saw anyone. One of the few people I would see was Noel, who would come for dinner round at my house, and I would sit there rattling from too many prescription drugs whilst he was at the other end of the scale! It was ironic that I missed the mad party that we had started with Creation when it went supernova. I watched it all sober whilst everyone else partied, and to be honest, watching them party made me feel good to be sober. Super-sober instead of supernova!

When I came back to Creation that year, I changed the way I ran the label. It was still a mad label – a fucking mad label – and everyone else was still caning it so there was not an immediate change in the culture. The characters were still there. I enabled that. I thought that it was particularly bonkers but our unique selling point was always signing the freaks – the normal people we signed never worked.

When I'd checked in to rehab, Oasis were just launching their debut single with a gig at the Wheatsheaf in Stoke on their first UK tour, and when I came out of rehab they were number 1. I had been off the drugs for months so that wasn't what I was in rehab for. I was there to try and find a way to get through life without all that. I had to learn to live at my own pace. I remember putting my head under the covers and just thinking, this is great. It was a relief. There was a lot of pressure on me at that point. It wasn't just the drugs. The label had also become a cult of personality at that point, which sounds ideal but brings its own issues.

Ironically, as I crashed, things were going great at the label. We had just put Primal Scream's 'Rocks' single out, and we had high expectations for Ride's third album *Carnival of Light,* and Oasis's debut album, and as far as the media was concerned it was all coming through this one individual, and that was me. I was watching Oasis breaking huge from a distance. I knew the singles 'Supersonic', 'Shakermaker' and 'Live Forever' had done well, and that the buzz was building for the debut *Definitely Maybe* album. The album went to number 1, and what should have been the culmination of everything I had worked for at the label happened when I was at my lowest ebb. This was *not* how to run a record label. It should have been my champagne supernova moment but I was burned out and drifting after my breakdown. I just couldn't enjoy the success at all. I had to leave my London penthouse – it was too much of a reminder of the past, and like a big empty party shell, same as me – so I moved into a hotel. I was truly the man who fell to earth.

I saw a lot of Noel in that period because he was living round the corner. Of course, he was having the time of his life in the fastest-rising band in the country, and jumping fully into the hedonistic rock 'n' roll lifestyle, whilst I was burned out by that life. He was buzzing at the scale and excitement of it all, and I was trying to get my head together. This was the bonkers thing about this period. The empire that I had built and the glorious moment that it created, I just couldn't enjoy. I couldn't go back to the office in Hackney as it had too many ghosts and memories of the life that I had left behind. I would walk miles around London on my own, building up my strength, getting fit and trying to get my head back into record-label mode.

The next step after my burnout was therapy. It was there that I faced all the demons and issues from my childhood onward that had driven me to this point. Those same demons that had engulfed and nearly destroyed me were the ones

226

that had driven me to make the record label such a success. I was thirty-five, with all this mad childhood stuff that I had no understanding of. Why I was beaten by my old man – I still didn't understand all that. In the therapy that I had, they were saying my father was an alcoholic who never addressed it and I was a recipient of his violence and that has obviously had an effect on me. Therapy taught me about myself. Like, it was not right for my father to jump on my head. It was not right to get beaten like that. I knew I was unlucky to have that happen to me, but I had never thought it was a big deal, but they said it created addiction issues. It was the bullying and violence of my old man, who was a thug to me over a sustained period from when I was eleven to sixteen. I never got bullied at school, I got bullied at home – school was easy compared to that. Therapy made me confront the difficult parts of my life. I started my long walks and losing weight, which I still do to this day. I stepped out of the indie world and into the real world beyond and wandered around and put things back into perspective – ironically, this is vital if you run a record label. Or want to continue to run a label. The music world is a bubble and you can get lost in that bubble.

Early Creation was just me and a couple of pals. It was a lot of pressure on very few people and something had to give. At first it was my personal life. It became even more stressful the bigger we got. Sometimes I just wanted somebody else to fucking help me with the big stuff at the label, but it seemed like I was the key to every situation. Maybe that was my fault, though. Everything was coming through me, and my way of dealing with that was drugs, fast drugs, and that kind of worked for quite a long time.

And then it didn't work. At the time I was probably emotionally too inadequate to deal with that level of success. I could have maybe done it without the drugs, but I just didn't have the life experience. My personality as a younger person was not developed enough to do it all sober, and so I just made the situation worse. It's the same with young bands. They often don't address situations and run away or medicate on drugs, and maybe I did as well.

Rehab saved my life. At the time I went to rehab we were running a really big operation out of a fucking broom cupboard with a very small team. It was the cult of McGee and it burned me out. Forty years later, I'm basically doing the same thing but I can handle it now and I work within my means and at my own pace. It took the breakdown to learn that.

CHAPTER 15

....

Staying motivated

Nothing lasts for ever. Bands have a golden period and then it just runs out. It's the same with labels. There are all kinds of reasons, but with Creation I think we just lost track. Every single person that worked for me in the early days was not there for their ability or how good they were at working in the music biz. They were working for me because, just like the bands, they were great characters and utterly loyal, and they were obsessed with music and would try their hardest. That's all that mattered. And it worked very well. Then towards the end, it was different. It became about ability. It became about this person being really good at the internet, or that person being really good at marketing, and the whole label became like that. It was professional, of course, but boring. It could have been Go! Discs or one of those bigger indie labels. Every record we released in the end just became one of these slick campaigns. In some ways, it had got too pro. Too good. But it sucked the life out of the label.

Maybe I was naive when I said that it was getting too slick. Maybe I regret making that remark but it's true. The people originally at the label would party all weekend and then somehow come back into the office on the Monday. Some of them had not even managed to get home and were still in the office from Friday after a 48-hour bender but they still picked themselves up to do their work on the Monday. It was like a gang. A crazy gang.

When I went back to the label after my burnout in 1995, I had changed, and then the label had to follow. The old Hackney office had been a riot but that couldn't go on forever. It was getting broken into all the time, and the days of cocaine piled up on the desk and the mad parties were over. It's vital that a label spend some time on the front line being bonkers, but it can't remain there forever, sadly. So we moved the office to Primrose Hill and it was hopefully a new start and a new chapter for me. I was much more open about my burnout and the fact that, now I was straight, Creation was going to have to be straight. So maybe I started the change. Hackney had been like *Scarface*, but the new office was a totally different experience. There was no drugs or booze in the office. Dick Green was happy about this as he was always much more into the work ethic. The new Creation started here, and whilst it was vital, it may have led to my eventual disillusionment with the label.

Like every label, there are different periods. Ebbs and flows. We had our days of indie pomp with the Valentines, Teenage Fanclub, The Boo Radleys and Ride, and then of course it went supernova, but since I had been in rehab there had been some problems. Ride's third album, *Carnival of Light*, had been a comparative flop, selling only 10,000 copies, which was a big disappointment after the huge numbers of their first two albums. Primal Scream had burned out touring America with Depeche Mode in 1994 – I think they were shocked by the hedonism of the headliners, who were already on what is now referred to as the Most Debauched Tour Ever and had added Primal Scream to the last thirty dates. That tour was crazy and Primal Scream were dangerously burned out trying to keep up.

Sony were also throwing their weight around and had forced us to drop a clutch of bands, like Adorable, The Telescopes and Dreadzone. If it hadn't been for Oasis the whole label would have got the chop, but they had the fastest-selling debut album in the UK so that meant we had some control left. It was at this point in 1995, when I wasn't sure about the label, that Noel played me a demo of three new songs that he had written – 'Don't Look Back In Anger', 'Wonderwall' and 'Morning Glory' – and I knew then that they had truly cracked it and we had the biggest album of the decade on our hands. It's moments like this that make running a record label worth it. That moment when an artist you felt were going to be not just great but the greatest actually delivers the goods.

But Team Creation was changing. When you run a record label you all have to be on the same wavelength. During the wild years, Tim Abbot was very much the core of the label with me and Dick Green. He was total rock 'n' roll and we were very much in cahoots. Now I had to get my act together and Tim was still living the life. He had left to join Oasis as a full-time freelance managing consultant, and had done a great job marketing *Definitely Maybe* when I was away. He had reached out beyond the music press and put ads in football and dance magazines, and match programmes, and had taken Creation to a whole new audience. He totally got it. Of course, we remained friends and Tim himself cleaned up in 2003 and became a cognitive therapist. Maybe it made sense to change the direction of the label now and then to keep it fresh. Whatever it was, I had no choice. But it just didn't feel right.

***

The new Creation was initially quite strange. People who worked in the office had to get used to a sober McGee. It wasn't just that I was sober after the breakdown, I was far less aggressive and people seemed to like me more. Add to this new mix the fact that Oasis were about to become the biggest group in the world and I didn't need the cocaine anymore. This was far more exciting.

We hadn't given up on the good times completely; they were just more organised and less self-destructive. Now that we were the hottest label in town, it was time to live like the hottest label in town. Growing up in the shadow of the swinging sixties, it felt great to have our own version. We employed Meg Mathews, who eventually married Noel Gallagher, as our 'artist liaison', which in reality meant turning what had been our ramshackle parties in the old Hackney office into the best parties in town. Meg's job was to invite the right people and make the parties really swing. Because of her we now had the sexiest parties in London in top locations with an A list of guests. There were people like Kate Moss, who were A list but also rock 'n' roll and understood our world. The guest list was cool, hip and the sort of people who got our scene. Creation was now sexy!

It wasn't just an upgrade from the shambolic Hackney offices with their attendant drink and drugs culture. The label itself was like a proper label now, with a marketing department, which, ironically, I hated – and a smooth operation. But this was not the music business I liked. The people who worked there were fine, but the dangerous spirit that had been such a big part of Creation was gone. The label ran itself with a new team who were as clean as the swanky new Primrose Hill office. A lot of this was probably driven by Sony, who were keen for a more professional setup than we had before.

I would not choose to run a record label without that maverick spirit, but then the whole music scene was no longer maverick. The very thing that made us also broke us. Indie had once been underground, but the minute Oasis broke it became a genre and not a spirit.

We killed indie. We had broken the barriers and made indie mainstream. It was no longer underground but in the stadiums. It was our fault. Oasis were accidentally destroying the culture. The huge success of the band had dwarfed the rest of Creation. They were the biggest band in the world and at first that felt brilliant, but as more and more people were brought in to work on them, the rest of the label became engulfed by their success and it created a weird schism in the office between the Oasis camp and the Creation camp. The other bands like Teenage Fanclub and Primal Scream, who were big bands in their own right, were feeling sidelined by what was happening, and justifiably so. They were still having big records but Oasis were supernova. The thrilling rush of Oasis taking off had sowed the seeds for what could be the end of Creation.

It was always going to be a strange situation, running an indie label through a major like Sony. They were quite different worlds but somehow we made it work. It was a necessity, as an indie label alone would not have been big enough to achieve the success that we had. It was a beautiful idea to be purely independent, but in reality this meant we were just a small corner of a massive battlefield. We were in a different world now. And it was not just us. By 1996, music was a whole different thing. Oasis cleaned up at the Brits and insulted everyone as they collected their awards, which was hilarious. They were now on the plateau and the only band up there with them was U2. All Noel's talk in the pub from a couple of years before had come true. Maybe he wasn't bluffing after all.

Oasis were now beyond the music press. *NME* and *Sounds* had been replaced by the tabloids, and Noel and Liam were never out of them. They were perfect for a label. Not only did they write great songs but they had a nose for a headline, and it wasn't even by design. There was no filter with Oasis; the way they spoke and the way they behaved was totally natural and created headlines at every turn. What had once been a world of fanzines like Communication Blur, Attack On

Bzag, Rox and The Legend getting sold out of plastic bags, was now Piers Morgan coming in to meet me and Andy Saunders, Creation's head of press, to tell us that the *Mirror* was going to go gung ho and fully support us. At that point, though, we were way past even that. Creation had sold 22 million Oasis albums. We were bigger than the press and we didn't want to be in the tabloids anymore. We didn't like the way they worked and that whole tabloid culture. That was really underlined after the *News of the World* pulled the lowdown stunt of bringing Noel and Liam's estranged father to their hotel in Dublin when they were on tour and making them meet him, which after a history of beatings in their youth and not seeing him for years was really snide. After that, the barriers were thrown up and the band were surrounded by a ring of steel of PRs and security.

My new head of press Andy Saunders had attitude and I liked that. He would say what he thought, even if it was hurtful, and the press didn't like it. I guess if we'd been running a label properly we would have toed the line and tried to make friends with the press, but that wasn't our way. There was one time when a newspaper in London got upset by his attitude towards them, so they wrote to me saying that I should sack him. This was a red rag to a bull because the kind of attitude that he had was what was missing from everything. Andy showed me the letter they had sent, which

I thought was hilarious, so I wrote 'Fuck off' on it, signed it and Andy wiped his arse on it and sent it back to them. It was gross but what could they do? Not write about Creation or Oasis? Andy liked to cause trouble and was out of control until he, like me, cleaned up. He certainly calmed down a bit after that but he was still fearless, and that, for me, is key to running a record label like Creation.

After the *News of the World*'s stunt, Oasis's press situation was never as good again and there was little we could do about it. We were now operating outside the music world, in the mainstream, which played dirty and so we had to learn fast. We were also now operating in a very different business world. The relationship with Sony had hit a major snag. They were stalling on the shares and I was wondering why. Jeremy Pearce at Sony just didn't seem to want to talk about the future of Creation. I eventually found out that he had been talking to Richard Branson, who wanted to set up a new label called V2 in 1996 after selling Virgin Records to EMI for a colossal amount of money. He wanted me and Dick to run the new label. The idea was that we would sign some new bands and maybe bring Oasis over for the UK only. If we had done this it would have meant the end of Creation. We were initially interested in the idea and went to talk to Richard Branson, who looked like the Queen Mother sat there in his woolly jumper. Despite that, I really liked and got on with him. The problem – which was understandable – was that Oasis would never have moved. If it ain't broke, don't fix it was their attitude, and they were right. The two albums on Creation through Sony had been massive – why would they move to a new label like V2?

V2 was more of an interesting idea than anything else. So I went back to Sony and asked them for a proper deal and a new four-year contract, but for some reason they were still stalling. Running a label is full of these life-changing choices, these endless forks in the road. Big day-to-day decisions. Maybe I should have gone to Virgin and taken Creation with me and Sony could have kept Oasis, who were easily their primary interest. It would have been good for me to go to the new V2 setup – a lot of money was involved and a big war chest was available to sign new bands. It was time for some brinkmanship.

I've always taken risks – for me that is integral to business, and especially the music business. You have to stand your ground and be prepared to lose everything. I wanted more respect and more backing from Sony, and they were stalling, so I made a statement about Sony to the press via an *NME* journalist with Andy Saunders taping it. We were not messing around and we were not bullshitting. Part of the statement said, 'Creation is an A&R company. The moment I let some fucking corporate arsehole in New York run the record company, I will resign, but it seems as if they are refusing to negotiate, and seem to be saying that they don't want me and Dick at Creation. We are Creation. If we go then I believe most of the artists and senior staff at the company will want to leave.' As expected, Sony hit back, saying they were going to buy Creation for 12 million – it was all made up of course, and part of the tit-for-tat positioning. I liked this kind of brinkmanship. It was the Glasgow street fighter in me. Going nose to nose. Sometimes you have to do this when you run a record label. Our next move was to go to the *Financial Times* with a story about the troubles at Creation and how the bands were worried about the situation, and we wondered if Sony could afford another court case like the then-recent one with George Michael.

Finally, after all this, we had their ear, and the boss Paul Russell sat down to negotiate properly. Because I had made a stand and because I could turn being difficult up to eleven out of ten, Sony backed off. They had the right to buy, but they knew that I held the keys to their credibility. They had tried threats but I had grown up on the streets of Glasgow and my father had also told me not to reply to threats. In the meantime, I could fire over a few threats of my own and bluff that Oasis would leave the label if they fucked with me – of course that would never have happened, but Sony couldn't be sure of that, could they? Marcus Russell, being the Oasis manager, wasn't thrilled that the band had been used as a bargaining chip but Noel loved it. He would. That 'fuck the business side' was something he enjoyed and so was the brinkmanship. V2 had offered me millions, so I knew my worth and we stood our ground and stopped Sony buying us completely, and eventually got an eight-figure sum from them to keep things as they were. I was now a multi-millionaire and a long way from Mount Florida.

Now I could get back to the label side of things. A new phase for Creation was starting. Dick had brought in a guy called Mark Bowen in 1995 to do the A&R, and he found Super Furry Animals, who were from Wales, same as him. For me, Super Furry Animals were the last great band that Creation signed. They were totally different and totally genius. I remember going to the Camden Monarch in 1995 to see them play in that tiny back room down there. They were supporting Powder, whose singer was Pearl Lowe, but were out there on their own and not part of any post-Britpop scene. The sound was terrible as it usually is was for support bands, but Super Furry Animals were was magical. Mark had told me they sang some songs in Welsh, and I said to them it would help sales if they sang in English and Gruff Rhys, their charismatic singer, and one of those characters that I always loved, told me that he was singing in English that night and that the PA was so bad I couldn't even tell.

I thought they were going to be my Blur, but they had their own thing going on. They were totally quirky and out there but somehow pop. I didn't get too involved with them and left most of the decisions to Dick and Mark. The only time I got involved was when I found out that they were going to put 'The Man Don't Give A Fuck' on the B side of a single and I insisted that it had to be the A side – what was everyone at the label thinking by hiding it on the B side? This was Creation! We embraced those kinds of titles!

What I loved about the bands was that they were more maverick than I was. For promo they asked us to buy them a tank instead of the usual round of paid-for ads. It got them press but, to be honest, I just loved the idea of the band driving around in a tank. This was more like the old days of Creation. The music biz was becoming really boring and full of dry accountants and business suits, so a sense of mischief was crucial. That had been a big part of running the label – the creative anarchy. It sometimes backfires but it sometimes strikes gold. The creativity isn't just writing the songs, it's in the way you run the business.

Despite Super Furry Animals' maverick approach reminding me of why I loved doing this, I still had niggling doubts about the label. Creation was a label run by the heart more than the head – that was its genius. In the later stages Creation was very successful but it was a different beast. It would have been easy for me to let this continue but I still had a nonconformist heart. That said, when fame and fortune had finally happened, I was determined to enjoy it. Then it went sour. I think I had my head up my arse for a while because I wasn't on drugs. Fame doesn't do most people any good. I think fame and fortune blew Bobby's mind, but then he came back to being Bob and that really worked. We all had to go through it and deal with it and none of us were taught how to. We were just kids at the time. Unbelievably, the Gallaghers had no problem when they became supernova famous, and were pretty unaffected by it all, and that is remarkable when you think about the level they got to.

When Oasis were the biggest band in the world I was living the high life without the highs. I was out of rehab, clean and I was enjoying it. I was living the good life. I would use the Sony limo. Why not? Oasis and Creation were paying for all of it, so why not have a few perks with the job. I had my own box at Chelsea and knew all the players, like Ruud Gullit, Gianluca Vialli, Ally McCoist and Pat Nevin. I had shares in Chelsea and would go to the matches, then afterwards we would all get in the limo and go to a club and they would drink champagne and I would sit there with my Diet Coke. The more Sony gave me, the more I asked for – who wouldn't? Maybe those were the last days of the decadence of record labels, that long-lost seventies world of

Led Zep having their own plane type of decadence. That kind of wild glamour. It was the working-class dream. If I asked for a helicopter to go somewhere, one would be provided. It was insane. There was now so much money going around that whatever I asked for I could get. They must have hated it, but I had given them Oasis and Sony were raking it in. They must have thought I was mad, but this was the part of running a record label that I could only dream about on the streets of Glasgow in my teenage years.

I even got over my post-breakdown fear of flying by taking Concorde to meet Sony in the USA. I hadn't flown since the breakdown and it was quite an experience. For three grand, you got a tiny, cramped plane that flew so fast it felt like it was going to rattle itself to pieces mid-flight. Not ideal for someone in my post-breakdown state but it got there, and fast. I was going to New York to meet Sony boss Tommy Mottola, whose name sounds like he's from a gangster film. Which is quite apt as he is quite an intimidating character in real life. Even his office was also straight out of a gangster film. You knock on the door and he opens it with a zapper, without standing up, and he's sat there behind a massive desk. It was just like the way you would imagine these guys do business. I loved those kinds of meetings though, but it felt like those days were over.

The music business was changing. Perhaps I was the last of the mavericks, the outsiders; the people that had got in during punk when the corporates had taken their eye off the ball. By the mid-nineties music was becoming more controlled and more commercial. The world of guitar bands, where I had made my life, was getting pushed aside. The big Britpop boom was over and the bands were not on the radio anymore. It was moving towards Spice Girls and pure pop and dance.

I had broken Oasis into the mainstream and it had been massive, but already we were living in different times. What had worked a few years before was not working now. I tried all the same tricks that I had used for Oasis to break Hurricane #1 into this new world, and it was like hitting a brick wall. The band were great. They had formed after the end of Ride when Andy Bell had built a new band around singer Alex Lowe. They had the songs and the attitude and I felt something could happen with them. We got off to a good start with a 1997 Paul Oakenfold remix of 'Step Into My World', which went into the charts at number 19, whilst the debut album had gone in at number 11 and sold 100,000. Would this be the base from which to move the band up to a bigger level? I mean, it was a success, but in the Oasis era of fame and fortune it felt small. In the new more volatile post-Oasis scene, bands were no longer the main currency in the culture. It only took one misstep for things to unravel.

* * *

Being in charge of a record label you have to make a lot of decisions and some of them can be plain wrong. In 1998 I advised Hurricane #1 to let their song 'Only The Strongest Will Survive' feature on an advert for the *Sun*. The money offered would pay to record the next album so it was good business but, looking back now, the loss of credibility at being associated with the *Sun* probably killed their career. It was a harsh lesson in the balancing act you have to play as an indie label. One wrong decision can fuck everything up. If you get too indie it just doesn't work, and if you get too corporate it taints the indie eyes. At its peak Britpop had been huge. In 1995 Cast had sold a million copies of their debut album *All Change*, but Hurricane #1 were just too late to make something of that huge new world that Oasis had created.

The peak and pinnacle was the two Knebworth Oasis gigs in August 1996 were the high point of the label, and should have been the endpoint. We should have stopped the label there like The Beatles in 1970. It was off the scale: 2.6 million people applied for tickets – reportedly 5 per cent of the British population at the time. The band could have sold out the venue for two weeks solid. In the end, Oasis played to 125,000 people a night – that's a quarter of a million people in total. It was the high water mark of the band, the label and the scene – where do you go next? As Liam said years later, 'It's like, what do you do when you've done everything?' Maybe I should have been like Paul Weller and The Jam and walked away at this peak. There could be nowhere to go after this, and if I was doing this for pop art perfection, then I would have walked away from the label there and then. My psychedelic punk dream that had started in the small back rooms of pubs and limited-edition singles was now selling 300,000 tickets for Knebworth with millions more who could not get in. I had proved a point. I had run an indie label that had turned into a tidal wave. We had started off as a cult and now we were the biggest in the country.

For a high point, the gig itself wasn't fun. It was far too big. I couldn't even get into my own hospitality tent because there were so many people there. There were liggers everywhere and people from way outside of our world running around the backstage area. It was a statement gig, not a rock 'n' roll gig. Noel had a point to prove and he really proved it. Oasis were the biggest band in the land and now everyone could see it. So, yeah, Knebworth would have been the perfect ending. A beautiful moment. I had the money, the kudos and the place in history. I had everything, but people still really wanted Creation. So we carried on.

CHAPTER 16

....

Don't mix
business and politics

When I came out of rehab in 1994, my head was a lot clearer. I was more focused in many ways. This meant a few things. I suddenly realised there was a world beyond the music and drugs that I had been immersed in since I was a teenager, and I was also a lot easier to be with. When I was on the drink and drugs I thought people wanted me to be mental so I would act mental. Then, after some time, it stopped being an act. I would be on 24/7 and it ran me into the ground. It certainly helped make Creation, but it wasn't doing me any good.

Now that I was clean and no longer mental, people seemed to like me. Just for being me. I was getting invited round to people's houses and I was talking to people and even listening to what they had to say. This was so different from the party days. I was suddenly connected to people and not ranting and raving like a loon.

I also started to look at the world beyond music and drugs and engage with it again. Drugs make everything very much about yourself, but now I was looking outwards. Part of this process saw me become a member of the Labour Party. This was noticed in Labour circles, and Derek Draper, who was then a Labour Party lobbyist, got in touch and asked if I was interested in meeting the party. So I thought, why not?

Politics had always been there, of course. I grew up in Glasgow and political defiance was part of the culture there. It was a working-class, left-wing city. Politics had also been a part of punk, with groups like The Jam and The Clash, but it took Oasis being the biggest band in the country before politics found me. Of course, politics was always around Creation. Bobby Gillespie's father was a big trade union guy and had stood for Labour in Glasgow in 1988 and lost to Jim Sillars from the SNP in a watershed by-election. Bobby had politics in his blood. It was always part of his being. I'm not a communist like him, but I'm left of the Tory party by a long way.

DON'T MIX BUSINESS AND POLITICS

At the 1996 Brit Awards, Tony Blair made a speech where he said that 'British music is in its rightful place, back at the top of the world.' It was like a big hint. Here was this youthful new leader of the Labour Party, who seemed to have a feeling for pop culture. He seemed to be connected with it. He might have been in a prog band at public school but he felt closer to our world than the usual lot. The night of his speech, Oasis won the Best Band award and gave Tony a shout-out from the podium. Noel Gallagher said, 'Seven people in this room give a little bit of hope to the young in this country. That's me, our kid, Bonehead, Guigsy, Alan White, Alan McGee and Tony Blair. And if you've all got anything about you, you'll get out there and shake Tony Blair's hand. He's the man. Power to the people!' Oasis were getting so big in 1996 that they had a voice and people listened. It felt like things were changing – not just in music but in the whole country. There was a wave of optimism. We had changed music, now maybe we could change the world. Or at least our bit of it. Could we harness our power to this? That would really be something for a record label to do.

Just after Knebworth, in August 1996, I was at home in London and Margaret McDonagh, who two years later would become the General Secretary of the Labour Party, called me. She asked if I was that McGee guy and if I wanted to join the party. I told her I'd already joined the party but hadn't got my membership card yet. So she says she'll be right round with it and comes over to my place with two other people and gives me the card. Door-to-door service! I invited them in and she then asked if I would be up for helping the Labour Party in the upcoming election and I said okay. Just to show how far away the political world was from understanding the music world, she also asked if I could get Oasis to play the 1996 Youth Party Conference in Blackpool on the upcoming Saturday. Or if Noel could come to the conference and present Tony Blair with a platinum disc on stage. This was on the Monday. No chance. Bands have mad schedules. Madder than even politicians. Noel had just got back from tour and was knackered. So I said I would go up and present Tony Blair with a platinum disc for *Morning Glory* instead.

Instead of Oasis playing, we sponsored the youth event. I wasn't just throwing money around for the sake of it. I wanted the Tories out and I was just doing my bit. At the same time, I also wanted to get more involved and push on issues such as unemployment in the music industry, to try to change policy. And if I was going to get more involved, I wasn't going to be a passenger. The following weekend I went up to Blackpool with Ed Ball and Andy Saunders to a special event for young Labour members at the Norbreck Castle Hotel. We also brought one of our bands, 18 Wheeler, to come and play as well. This was the same Aberdeen band that had played that now famous Glasgow gig where I had signed Oasis a few years before.

It was my first political do and I didn't know many people there. All I remember was that Waheed Alli and Steve Coogan were also at the event and they were the only faces I recognised. During the night, Tony Blair walked in with his huge grin and I went on stage and gave him the disc. He then introduced the band as 'Wheeler 18' and then they played and there was a boring party afterwards. I slipped out because I was still fresh from rehab and wasn't doing parties then, so I went back to my hotel and put on the TV and there I was giving Tony Blair the disc. That night I was on every channel constantly. This was the kind of publicity you could not buy at a record label. I was now in a very different world.

After Blackpool, I donated £100,000 to Labour and they began to invite me to more meetings and I got to know some of the key players, like Alastair Campbell. I got on with him as well as Tony Blair. These days no one has anything good to say about Tony, but this was before the Iraq War and where it all went wrong. Things were different back then. I was hanging around with Margaret McDonagh more and more and getting more into politics. I gave Labour money, and she explained that being involved with Creation gave the Labour Party a sense of the now. I went to Millbank with her and

Peter Mandelson and they showed me the campaign videos and told me the campaign song was going to be D:Ream's 'Things Can Only Get Better', which I told them was a shite choice. I said it should be 'Wake Up Boo' by The Boo Radleys, but that never happened because they obviously had no idea about pop culture. In hindsight, maybe if they had listened to all of my ideas, that would have been the best use of me and the label.

Not that they were clueless. The best thing they did was make the 1997 election a Britpop moment. They caught the wave. The youthful optimism of Britpop created a feel-good pop culture landslide. They got a dose of cool from us and we managed to align Oasis with them, which helped them win the election. It all made sense. Tony Blair had a rock 'n' roll past and I had the biggest band in the world. I was bringing Noel Gallagher to the party and we had aligned Oasis to Labour and Tony Blair was very grateful.

The 1997 election night was unreal. The atmosphere was like a gig. It was euphoric. The highlight was when Michael Portillo lost his seat. When that happened it was the loudest roar I've ever heard. It was louder than an Oasis gig or the football. That was a rock 'n' roll moment. There was a big feeling of optimism and that euphoria carried on into the early days of New Labour. Eventually, though, I realised that politics probably works in just the same way as the big record companies at a top level. It's not like punk. Unfortunately.

At first, after the election, I was getting more and more involved. I was appointed to the Creative Industries Task Force along with Richard Branson, Paul Smith and other business bigwigs. They wanted me to be the leader of it, which would have kinda made me the head of the music industry in all of Britain. I turned that down because I preferred being on the team and not the leader and changing the system. I might have been working with them but I was not part of the gang. Even in politics, I was still the indie guy. The outsider. I may have been running a big label with the biggest band in the UK on it, but I wasn't like the other music people involved in politics. I was not like Mike Smith, who was running EMI Publishing and was at the top of his game having signed people like PJ Harvey, Elastica and Supergrass, and who would go on to sign Gorillaz, White Stripes, The Libertines and Arctic Monkeys. Mike can play the corporate game and still be a left-field character. I could never play the corporate game, but I could do deals with those people and it was the same with the Labour Party. I could get things done without becoming part of their world.

The danger with politics is how they chew you up and spit you out if you come from the music world. Paul Weller had done the Red Wedge tour a decade before in support of Neil Kinnock's Labour Party, and it had backfired; despite its good intentions, it hadn't changed much. I was aware that I could end up being burned as well, but despite that, I was overruled in my head by my hatred of the Tories. Maybe it's a Glasgow thing or maybe it's because they really are cunts, but I thought that if I could do my little bit to help, then this was it. Admittedly I was naive about politics when I got involved. Saying that, though, they must have liked me because once they were in power they let me change policy. It was in meetings with them that I came up with the New Deal for musicians, which gave them three years to develop and be funded by the government instead of having to take other jobs to survive. It meant that musicians got off the dole and I helped enact a law that saw them get benefits.

The New Deal was a great thing. I did it with this guy called Stuart Washington who was from Manchester. It was legislation that provided support for unemployed musicians. For ten years after that, a kid who wanted to make music could simply show up with a guitar to the welfare office and collect fifty quid a week. I changed the law for the better. It was maybe one of the best things I've ever done in my life. It's certainly one of my proudest achievements. People like Chris Gentry from Menswear, or bands like The Libertines, were just a few of those that benefitted. It even helped some of the bands who I had worked with before. Stephen Pastel was one of the many tutors and mentors. A lot of people got money out of the scheme. The New Deal for musicians was me putting something back into music after a successful career. Maybe that's how to run a record label – not just release life-changing records but actually change lives.

Whilst politics was part of a lot of music, it wasn't central to Creation. We were doing things that were not purely music anymore; in some ways we had strayed off the path, and maybe politics was where we got out of our depth. Now I'm back on the music and that's it. That's my world. Looking back, I think the politics period was bizarre. Maybe we were getting big-headed and thinking we were better than we actually were. For many people this was encapsulated by the infamous moment when Noel and I went to 10 Downing Street to celebrate the 1997 election victory. It was a party to thank everyone who had supported Labour. Again, it was like stepping into another world. Even just the fact I'd been invited was big news. I was in the gym the afternoon before the party and saw them talking about me on the TV news on all the screens. That was a bit bizarre. They were saying Alan McGee will be asking Tony Blair some tough questions tonight, like they knew this for a fact. If I was going to be asking questions, it was the first I'd heard of it.

Afterwards, Noel and I got a lot of flack for going there, but I don't think it was justified. I wasn't sure about going at first, but to be invited was beyond anything I would have thought possible when I was younger. It was my wife Kate who persuaded me to take the invitation. She was right when she said you will never be able to know what it's like in 10 Downing Street because you will never be asked again. It was cool just to go and see what it was like. To have a nose around. And she was right, I've never been asked back. Despite the backlash we got afterwards, I'm glad I went. I like the idea of the likes of me and Noel looking around 10 Downing Street. I think it's funny. Of course, it was easier that they didn't invite Liam, because at that point in his life he was maybe too much of a loose cannon!

The whole night was pretty mad. Kate and I went round to Noel's place and we piled into his roller. When we got to Downing Street, it was mayhem. There was a media scrum and the flashlights were popping. It was then that I realised just how big this was, and how it was a pop culture moment, like when The Beatles met Harold Wilson at the height of the swinging sixties. It was a case of two worlds colliding at a place right at the heart of the mainstream. The whole night was a high water mark in UK pop culture. Or of Britpop and New Labour, or whatever you want to call it. Tony Blair winning the election was another Britpop moment. Maybe the ultimate Britpop moment along with Blur v Oasis. At the time, we all believed that Tony Blair was going to get the job done. It felt like all the things we had been doing were coming to fruition and that we really were going to see a revolution.

The Downing Street party was wall to wall people and faces, and other bands like the Pet Shop Boys were there. When I arrived I chatted with Tony Blair for about five minutes, and when he shook Noel's hand the cameras were flashing like crazy. That photo ended up everywhere. I remember all the MPs getting more and more pissed, and Jack Straw was talking to me and seemed to know a lot about cocaine, until Alastair Campbell came over and jokingly said to him 'Enough!' Alastair Campbell was not just checking on the politicians, he also made sure that the rock 'n' rollers didn't get too out of control. We had some bodyguard type on our case looking over our shoulders all the time, just in case.

The party was one of those moments that freeze-frames your life. For a brief moment, I thought, this is what running a record label is about. It was a long way away from when I had five pence and I was on the door at The Living Room, taking small amounts of money and putting on great underground bands. Thirteen years later, I'm in Downing Street telling them what to fucking do. Some journey. It was incredible. When we left, the cameras went crazy again, and then we went back to Noel's house and watched it on the news all night. It was a very surreal moment.

The music biz really had it in for me now, for getting too close to the politicians. I was on the *Today* show on BBC

Radio Four, and they did a whole piece about me working with the government. They got me on the show to say my piece. It was early morning and they didn't tell me that they had Bill Drummond from the KLF in to argue with me. I already knew Bill, of course – I had put out his solo album *The Man* on Creation in 1986, but I didn't know that he was going to be on and he took me to pieces. He really tore me apart about going to Downing Street. It was too early in the day for me, and the only person who would have been worse to argue with at that time would have been Malcolm McLaren. It was a nightmare.

It made me start to realise that maybe I was out of my depth. The ideas were good, but was I the right person to do this? Creation was now a cultural force, but I don't know if we did the right thing by going into politics. I still had enough vision to know that I had maybe lost my way, and I knew I had to reconnect with it, and if that meant tearing everything up and starting again, then I would do it. That was the punk rock part of me that never left. We should have maybe stayed on course as a label. I should have signed bands like Coldplay and the Foo Fighters and really gone for it, but that's not what I'm like. I like a curveball and going in another direction. Once I got into politics, that was my next journey for a bit. It was a strange world and it ended in a cul-de-sac.

Tony Blair had his vision of a 'Cool Britannia' that we were all now part of, and was creating this world of diverse people to be involved. It was a great vision to start with and I went to many of the events which were like another world for me and a long way from running an indie label. That was when it started to get really strange. In 1999 Tony Blair invited me for dinner at Chequers with people like former Celtic chairman John Reid, and Dame Judi Dench and her husband Michael Williams, and the Admiral who would have pushed the nuclear button at the time if there was a war.

This was a very different world from the one I was used to. When we got there in the limo there were SWAT teams on the lawn. Then Tony Blair and I had a ten-minute discussion about Blur and Oasis, and if that was not weird enough, then the final guest tipped it over the edge. I could hear someone going, 'Now then, now then,' and Jimmy Savile walked in with a security guy. I looked at Tony and said, 'This can't get any more bizarre,' and he burst out laughing. I had no idea what it was going to be like, and I certainly had no idea that Jimmy Savile would be there. Not only that, he was in full Savile mode, running around like he owned the place, complete with his annoying catchphrase. He was just plain weird, acting like he was the host rather than Tony Blair, speaking to the whole table like he was in charge. You could sense something really dark about him even then, when I didn't know he was a fucking paedophile or anything like that. This was before all that stuff had come out, but he was still a horror to be near throughout the meal. He had started to hit on Kate as she was sat between him and Judi Dench. He was kissing his way up her arms, kissing her fingers. Kate came over and said, 'He's a pervert,' and thankfully he left her alone once she was next to me. I was sat there, thinking, 'What a dirty old man.' I wanted to warn him off, Glasgow style, but at Chequers it's not the done thing to break someone's nose.

This was all a long way from running a record label. Too far. It was certainly a much weirder crowd than I had ever seen at the label or at any gig.

My relationship with music was shot once I got involved in politics. The music biz didn't mind me when I was a wee working-class guy from Glasgow who had sold 22 million copies of Oasis's *Morning Glory*. They thought I was an arrogant little prick, but I was successful and I made them and Sony and HMV loads of money, blah, blah, fucking blah. But when I ended up in government and almost in charge of the music business, the bigwigs got fucking pissed, man. It upset them because I was now above my station. I was all right acting large and making everyone loads of money – then they put up with me. But when I was in with

Richard Branson, Paul Smith and the others, and close to government, then the people who really ran the music biz were out to get me, and they eventually did. They didn't like the fact that I was so close to the politicians that they could get nowhere near. These guys were used to being the big guys in the establishment, and now I was the man, and that's when I overshot the runway. And once you overshoot the runway, you can't reverse the plane.

I got a lot of criticism for the Labour thing, but who else in the music biz has actually changed things? U2's manager Paul McGuinness made sure more gig money got paid to artists from the PRS, and there was me sorting out the New Deal for musicians who were struggling, and Tony Wilson with the Haçienda, and maybe a couple of others who had made actual change. The rest of pop and politics is great songs and hot air.

I eventually got disillusioned with politics. They only used me when they needed me, and in the end were not really listening to me. It had worked well for them, and the whole Cool Britannia and Oasis thing had given Tony Blair an extra shine to his aura and had helped deliver the youth vote and make them look cool. But I was getting a bit too establishment and that never sits well with me. It had got to the point where Prince Charles had invited me to lunch at Buckingham Place three times, but I never went because

I hate the royals. Maybe I should have gone just to see what he was like, but it's not really me.

It was at this point that I realised I was a long way from my world and maybe it was time to rein it all in. In 1999 I put Malcolm McLaren up for Mayor of London against Labour candidate Frank Dobson; that was what eventually drove the wedge between me and the Labour Party. They got fucking annoyed about that. They didn't like it and we sort of fell out but that's just me being me.

The mayor thing was great. It was classic Malcolm how he got me involved. Basically, he announced I was putting him up to be the Mayor of London without me even knowing. He trapped me! Once he'd said that there was no way out. It was like a challenge. Not that I was looking for one. I only found out when I was in the Caribbean on holiday and I heard through the grapevine. We had talked about him being mayor at one of our long dinners, but not me being involved. I never agreed to anything but he just announced it anyway. When I thought about it, though, I had to do it. It was such a great idea. This was what a record label should be doing! Something subversive and full-on pop cultural. Somehow I managed to get Sony to stump up the twenty grand for the mayoral campaign by telling them it was an art project. Which, in a sense, it was. Malcolm was full of great ideas about culture and music in a way that I wasn't,

DON'T MIX BUSINESS AND POLITICS

but he couldn't make a penny out of any of them. That was more my skill.

I enjoyed doing the campaign with him. I don't think even he thought he had a serious chance of winning, but it was a great platform for him and it also had the advantage of severing all ties between me and New Labour, which at that point was a good thing. Eventually, Malcolm stepped aside for Ken Livingstone, who was running as an independent against Labour's Frank Dobson and eventually beat him. After that, me and politics split.

For a brief while politics had given me the buzz I was missing, but that had now faded. These days I have no faith in the political system. The music business is bad enough, but politics is even worse. It's just a system run for its own benefit. Effective change is made by individuals, not the major parties who have their own agendas. I saw all this close-up; that the people who really run things are big business or other shadowy figures, or countries like America.

I don't think I was the right person ultimately for Labour. I don't play the game. They needed me briefly to help them win the election and beat the Tories, and that was enough for me. I'm an antagonist. I love upsetting people. That has been a core part of the way I run my life and my labels. It used to be that I'd upset Stephen Pastel. Now I was upsetting Peter Mandelson or Tony Blair. It was the same thing, but maybe with higher stakes!

So I went back to music, and they eventually got rid of Tony Blair. The whole Iraq War thing was the end of him, really, although I still like him. I still speak to him now and then. He contacted me not so long ago and we met at his office somewhere near Hyde Park. I had forty-five minutes with him and it was friendly but a bit odd. It was a long time after Iraq and a long time after Britpop. It was like two older guys meeting after all this mad shit and trying to make sense of it. It was all a bit, 'Don't Mention the War' like the *Fawlty Towers* sketch. He's not a bad guy. I think in another life he would've been in a rock band, but he ended up running the country, and I ended up running a record label instead of running the country.

CHAPTER 17

....

Know when to walk away

To this day I don't know if I made the right choice in closing Creation. I don't even know if I'm talking about the label as an aesthetic or a business thing. I could have kept the label going for another ten years and it would have been good, but personally, I think I did the right thing because I had a great next ten years. At the end, after Creation and the follow-up Poptones label, I was happy to get out and stay at home and do the family thing. It was like John Lennon's semi-retirement when he was baking bread in the late seventies. Sometimes you need that domesticity. That reality. In some ways, though, closing the label was a naive thing because it was like killing the goose that laid the golden eggs. On the other hand, every label should know its timescale. Its period. Creation could have spun out its success to the present day but it would have watered down the vision. You should know when to call it quits – as Paul Weller did with The Jam. Or The Beatles did when they didn't 'get back'. Go out at the top.

I'd done pretty well for a guy with no education and with no business people in my family. During the nineties the whole music world was becoming more and more structured and corporate. It was getting boring. At first I thought I could do that, I could deal with that new world, but in the end I was jaded to fuck. I wasn't enjoying it. You can become a business machine and lose the fire that made you, so I did the right thing for my head in the end. The biggest crime in music is to be boring. Or to be bored. And the label was getting boring.

By the end of 1996, I stopped going into the office. I was successful and the label was the hottest in the UK but I didn't feel anything for the people working there. It felt like they were from a different world. I bought another office round the corner so I didn't have to hang around at the main office. I guess that should have been a sign that things were not right. I shared the new place with Meg, who was married to Noel by then. She had set up her own promotion company and she was a good laugh and great to be around. I liked my new sanctuary and no one else was allowed in there apart from Bobby Gillespie and sometimes Dick Green. I was bored of the label and of the music biz. The madness that had been part of the thrill of running a record label was dying out. Not only were the professionals taking over but the very nature of the business was morphing into something I didn't like.

The internet was looming on the horizon, and if at first I didn't really get it and what it could do, when I finally had a look I was blown away. It was Kate who kept telling me about it, and one day I typed 'Oasis' into Google search and was stunned by what I saw. There was so much information and debate and noise going on online, and within an hour I was hooked. When I get into something I go in with both feet, and now I was down the internet rabbit hole. I saw the future and realised that the current model of running a record label was over. The internet was going to change everything. You could see it even then. The way people heard about music, the way people heard music. It was all going to change. Labels were not going to be about selling records anymore. Our culture was spinning on its axis. The old model of the music biz was now totally irrelevant. All this information was there at the touch of a button. It was the biggest change in culture and it was just starting. It was a revolution.

I like revolutions. I was a convert, and when I get converted I go the whole hog. I wrote an article in something like the

Guardian, predicting the end of the old music biz model because of the internet. I was saying things like having a record company, having a publishing company, having internet start-up companies, having a film company and having a management company is the future – it's multi-media, not being one-dimensional and having one record company. That had worked for the last twenty-five years, but it didn't make sense anymore.

Predictably, those in the music biz were not happy. No one (except me) likes the apple cart getting knocked over. Maybe they could see the future as well, and how it was a threat to all their jobs. They kinda knew what was going on but didn't want it or accept it. I don't blame them. They thought I was mad but they already knew what was happening and the following years proved me right.

The music biz was totally changing and Creation would have to change as well. Maybe it was sink or swim. Really it was what running a record label should be about – a vision of the future. Not treading water. The point of running a label is that you have to be current and not too lost in the past – like the 'rock 'n' roll collectors' that Malcolm McLaren used to talk about. There were other factors at play, too. Maybe I was fed up with making business decisions and had lost a little of the instinctive love of guitar music I grew up with? I had to remind myself why I was doing this. Sometimes it gets too comfortable. Whatever it was, it was important for me to step outside my comfort zone. Embrace a little danger.

At first I got involved in releasing more pop stuff for Creation, which was a long way from the indie guitar stuff we were known for. It was an experiment. A way to engage in something different. I released stuff like my wife Kate's band Client, who were making sublime electronic pop, but the singles stalled in the charts. It was hard to get them beyond cult status in the UK. Their songs were popular in the rest of the world but I just couldn't get them away in the UK. For a while, I also released Mishka, which people said was not right for Creation and was a flop, but it sold about 100,000 copies worldwide. It was interesting being involved in something different, but I was still restless. It was at that point that I thought it was maybe time to move on.

Putting the Kevin Rowland solo album out put me in touch again with the true feeling of running a record label – that it's about the music and the art. Some of the people working at the label didn't get the album or its artwork, and it was then that I knew the label was over. For me, releasing 'difficult' records is part of the art of running an indie label. You should never back away from the difficult stuff. Take risks. The kind of label I wanted to run had to deal with this stuff. The trouble was that I was now surrounded by people who didn't think like that. Proper old-school Creation was about not giving a fuck, and the art was a key driving force. Now more than half the office were music people who worked on Oasis because they were so big, and who were living in a world of corporate, mainstream indie.

The new generation thought indie meant only one thing – guitar bands – like it was a style of music, but for me it stood for independence. It wasn't a musical genre, it was an attitude. Like punk. That idea was part and parcel of labels like Creation. Or should have been. We had been born in a different era, forged out of punk, in a time when an indie label was a maverick operation, not just a genre of music sold by the majors. I could feel that many of the people in the Creation office didn't like the way I worked. They were part of this new indie world and seemed to resent that I still had the power to make bonkers decisions over the records. Some of the releases they didn't agree with. That was another sign that rock 'n' roll was getting boring. Was this what running a record label had become? I didn't want a safe label that was an extended arm of a major. I wanted something else, and the last few months of Creation had me rethinking what a record label should be.

The last release on Creation was a perfect curtain call. It was another uncompromising piece of work from Primal Scream, their new album *XTRMNTR*, which came out in January 2000. It was perhaps their best album and the perfect kiss-off to Creation. The album was dark. It was like a hangover from the acid house days. It's a genius album, and a great place to end the label, with the band that was core to what we once were. The record came out but Creation was already over for me. Exterminated. On the opening track, they sang about the money man losing his soul, and I wondered if they were singing about me. Maybe not, but it made me think.

I looked around the office and there were fifty people in there, and I wasn't sure I knew even half of them. A normal label would have been satisfied with this situation, but not me. I was safe now. I could have run a label like this for years and coasted it for the rest of my life, signing watered-down versions of our main bands. But this was not what I got into rock 'n' roll for. I still had a punk rock heart. There may have been fifty people in the office but I only ever spoke to five of them – Joe, Ed, Dick, John Andrews and Andy Saunders – it was almost like a mini Creation within an extended Creation. I didn't have any affinity with anyone else in there. This was not how to run an indie label.

One February morning in 1999 I rang Dick and told him what I thought, and that I was quitting. To my surprise, I found out that he agreed with me. We both felt it was over. Dick said that he had felt that way for five years, since the beginning of Britpop and since we had gone supernova. He felt the label had gone in a different direction since then.

Sony and its boss Paul Russell were not happy that I was quitting. I was ruining the golden egg. They called me up and tried to make me continue with a different model. They suggested stripping the label down and cutting back to the core of the staff and to the core of the label and keeping the big four big acts that I had at the time – Oasis, Primal Scream, Teenage Fanclub and Super Furry Animals – but my mind was made up. The Primals were not happy but I had to quit, even if Bobby was upset about it. He may not have run the label but, in some ways, he was the label. His spirit was part of the core of Creation and he still believed in what we were doing and what Creation was about. It was the same with Liam, who felt that I was abandoning him to the tabloids. Noel was more defiant. 'We won, they didn't,' he quipped.

The last release was going to be the fourth Oasis album, *Standing on the Shoulder of Giants,* in 2000, which would have been a great place to finish. But when I ended Creation they went straight off and set up their own Big Brother label to release it on. They had no choice really because the Sony accountants pulled the plug on the label even before we quit. Sony knew that the size of Creation and that amount of staff was unsustainable, and that the label was going to have to be shrunk, even if we'd carried on. Maybe I had sensed that as well and decided to close the label before they could. I tried to explain this to the staff when I shut the label – that the whole thing was now unsustainable and I had lost interest – but understandably they were pissed off. The twenty-four-hour party was over and Creation was no more.

Where do you go after running a record label? To a less stressful post at another label perhaps? Start a new label? Sit back and be a pundit like an old football pro? Go and make the easy money? I chose to opt out. It was time to take back the time. Bake bread. Read. I read a lot. I was immersed in some pretty left-field books and making sense of my life and who I was and the weird psychic stuff that happened around me. I enjoyed the quiet and the enigmatic status. For the first time in years, I found peace and lay low with my wife Kate and daughter Charlie, living as close to a normal life as I could.

Sometimes I would dip back into the music world. I would occasionally DJ or give talks on music in weird and wonderful parts of the world if the money was stupid enough. If you were my friend I would turn up and DJ just for fun. I was not looking for a job. I didn't have to. I'd done everything in music, or so I thought. I was down some very different rabbit holes now. I was trying to make sense of my own life instead of other people's.

CHAPTER 18

....

The ones that get away

R egrets? I missed a few. Even trusting my instinct and being open to things didn't mean I got every band. Maybe being off my nut for a few years got in the way, but I still managed to get most of the great bands of that time, so I don't have too many of those regrets. The story of any label is full of 'what if's. Creation is no exception. For every band I signed there were many I missed. You can't be everywhere all at once, you can't possibly get it right every time, and you can't have every single band.

The Stone Roses would have been great. They would have been a perfect Creation band, musically and style-wise – they were like the synthesis of everything we were looking for. If I'd run into them at the time I would have tried to work with them. I didn't know enough about them before they made it, despite Debbie Turner constantly tipping me off about this brilliant new band. I have always listened to what's going on as much as I can, but how can you track everything? The Stone Roses were my type of band and their debut album is totally genius classic. On that album every member of the band is at the top of their game. Every one of them is a fucking working-class hero rock 'n' roll star. Later on, in 1997, I nearly worked with Ian Brown when he was going solo. Mani set up a meeting with me and Ian and I was going to sign his first solo album but for various reasons the meeting didn't work out.

I also missed signing Suede in 1991. They were around at the point in time when I was actually thinking that I was actually really fucking talented and some kind of record company genius and music guru and could turn everything into gold. I was thinking, I'm Alan McGee and I know what's what! I was lost in the hype. It makes me laugh now, thinking about it. It was because of that stupid attitude that I didn't want to sign them. I was thinking I was bigger than all of that. Bigger than the bands! And I was above all that. I still don't know why I didn't go for Suede. I was so conceited at the time; I thought I was so completely different and I knew best. I regret missing out on them.

There have been some even bigger misses than that. I turned down the Foo Fighters despite their manager John Silva handing them to me on a plate. It was like I was just not even fucking interested when I heard they were looking for something. I was at the football watching Chelsea play Crystal Palace in 1998. I was with Russell Warby, who is a Palace fan and the agent for the Foo Fighters. He turns around to me and goes, 'McGee, Grohl loves you. They're fed up with EMI, why don't you sign them?' And I said to him, 'They are not cool enough for me!' Russell hates me telling that story and he has screamed at me down the phone for doing so because he thinks it makes the Foo Fighters look uncool, but I'm telling it the other way round – it makes me look like a fucking idiot. Because I turned down the one band from that genre that sells out fucking football stadiums! Maybe they would not have fitted or worked on Creation. They are not a cool band in the Creation sense, I suppose. I've met David Grohl a few times since then and he's a nice guy. He sent me his book a few years later and we have talked, but they were not really a Creation band. It was a different thing. A different aesthetic.

Another band that I should have signed was Spacemen 3. I was obsessed with their *Perfect Prescription* album and wanted to put the next record out, but in 1987 Creation was not a big thing and they signed with Fire Records instead. Maybe it would have worked out better for them if they had signed to Creation. Maybe we could have helped them stay together instead of falling out. Who knows.

One of the things about signing bands to a record label is that they have to fit with the aesthetic of the label. That's important no matter how big the band is. What makes a label and what made Creation was that we always believed in the bands we signed, whether they were big or small. When you run an indie label, it has to be your vision. You can't just sign random bands. That makes no sense at all.

The band I would have really loved to have worked with were Television Personalities, because that was the band that inspired me to do all of this in the first place. I wish I could have signed them. They certainly needed someone who didn't just get the music but knew how to do the business for them as well. I could have really made something work with Dan and the band. I wish more people knew about his genius. That was another big part of Creation – getting the spotlight onto these outsider geniuses. Paying them back in a sense. Embracing their brilliance.

CHAPTER 19

∙∙∙

The art of being a manager

These days I'm running down the record label side of things and becoming a full-on manager. Managing bands is not new to me – I was Primal Scream's manager up to 1992, and managed Saint Etienne in the early nineties as well. When we got hold of the Mary Chain in the beginning no one wanted to manage them, so I did it. I didn't want to be a manager but I became their manager. I was naive but that was also an advantage. I was so naive that I tour-managed the Mary Chain too, because I thought all managers did that. I was actually the tour manager on that first American tour in a splitter van. I understood how it felt. I had been there. After eight weeks you understand what it's like to be in a band touring America – it's fucking hard, but the insight was invaluable when it came to running a record label. Ian Copeland was the agent in America – he was Miles Copeland's brother – who ran FBI touring and booked the tour. We got told by Warners to come, and against everyone's advice we went to play there on a budget and it was totally successful. The total income was 15,000 dollars from the ten shows we played in December 1985, but we made money because I was the tour manager. We came back with a couple of thousand dollars in profit, which was unheard of at the time at that level of touring. That's a measure of how naive we actually were – we didn't blow the money on big-budget touring like everyone else. I was a kid. I didn't know the rules. I made my own fucking rules. I always have done.

I like the business side of management, but it's also really creative. These days, management's becoming much more of my main role. The nature of the music business has changed and what I want to do has changed. Getting a band on the road and plotting their career is the key now; selling records is less important. These days a record label is a different beast. In the era of downloads and the internet, the role of the label has been reduced. But the skills I picked up from running Creation are perfect for being a manager. The recent labels I had been running, like Poptones or Creation 23, don't really exist anymore. They helped to make a couple of records for young bands, to get them started. In truth, it's all about the management now.

Being hands-on as a manager is really important, but I can do that anywhere. I don't need an office. Tech has revolutionised the way I work. You can be remote now. In the late seventies, we had no choice but to relocate to London. Now I can be anywhere in the world and still be in touch with everything. The internet has made sure of that. I can be in Spain for two weeks in the sun, kicking about in Youth's studio, booking stuff, sorting out interviews and dealing with agents. Or I can walk the streets of London or be sat on a train going to my artists' gigs and I can still manage a lot of what is going on. I'm always moving. I don't keep still. I don't think you can be a good manager and be stuck in an office all day.

Also, we live in very different times from when we started out. I'm aware that because of Instagram and social media, what you look like is crucial. And it's not just the bands but the managers as well. The visuals are as important as the music now. I lost a load of weight over the pandemic lockdown because I was walking everywhere. I was the only person on the streets of London, walking around doing my deals on my phone. Getting in shape is important now. I think that the way you look is monumental to people's perception of you. I don't look washed up and it helps. If I looked like a cunt, people would swerve me. I look good now. I was skinny for forty years, and then I got fat for twenty years, and then I got skinny again and suddenly people think I'm really on it. Bands also know it's about the look as well as the music. Rock stars usually have to be skinny, so I got in shape mentally, physically and culturally. I had no choice, really, because all that walking around London gets you into shape.

These days, after the books and the film about Creation Records, people know me. It's not the same level of fame as Shaun Ryder; he can't go anywhere without an avalanche of selfies, whereas I get a handful. I went to see The Rolling Stones recently, and Shaun asked if he could come. He was in Manchester and asked for a ticket for the London show. I said, Shaun, what you don't understand is that if you come and I'm in with the punters, you will have a nightmare. You're on the telly every week and everyone knows you. A few people might recognise me and ask for a selfie, but five hundred people will want your selfie during the first Stones song and you will get pissed off and won't see any of the gig because you're that well known. That's the difference in levels of fame. Mine, I can handle easily.

As a manager, I look after classic bands now. Vintage bands. I'm working with legends who need a bit of care and attention. I'm the king of the oldies. King of the analogue. I have my roster of bands that I manage and it's at capacity, but the older bands keep coming to me to manage them. They know I've done this for years and I know all the tricks. They have seen what I can do and how I can make their bands feel vital again. They call me up and I go and tweak their careers and make them shine again. It's a bit like Harvey Keitel in *Pulp Fiction* – I'm the fixer. I still get intrigued with the characters in the older bands; they still shine, decades on. When you have that kind of charisma it's always there, you never lose it. My job is to make sure people can see and hear it. You get that bit right and the band works again. What made the older bands great when they were younger is still lurking in there. Some are even in danger of turning into national treasures. Who's the most unlikely person to become a national fucking hero? Shaun Ryder... but it's what he fucking should be. And that's not because I made it happen. I just moved a couple of things around. It's Shaun who is the national treasure. He just has that thing. I just need to make sure people see it. He's my pal and I have managed him for a few years, in which he has gone from being a drug addict to a national fucking favourite, but that was all him. It's the way he is. In music, people relate to him because he's a genius. In real life, people relate to him because he's funny, engaging and wise.

A lot of bands ask me to be their manager. If I'm interested, I come in and have a look at what needs to be done. Of course,

I attend to the business side, but I can also get involved creatively and advise on what kind of gigs they should play and how they should run their careers. It's the same sort of thing you would do with younger bands if you signed them to your label, but these bands are not looking for their first big break or their first big hit. They are looking to work with what they already have, or had, and make it work again. And they trust me to do that.

People often ask what I do to change the bands I manage, to rejig their trajectory. I always tell them it's simple. All I did with The Jesus And Mary Chain was turn up the volume. They had got all safe, and William was not using feedback anymore. It was getting tame. I went to Paris for the 'Psychocandy' tour, when they were playing that classic album again, which is a move I always encourage, as well as making them write new songs again. Jim said the gigs were not working for some reason and the album didn't feel the same, so I went to the mixing desk and I mixed the sound. All I did was turn it up, and people were saying it was the loudest gig they had been to in thirty-five years, and the band sounded urgent, and that underlined what they needed to do, which was to get loud and get dirty.

When I work with a band now, I look at the big picture. In many ways it's like when I ran the label – I try to keep pretty hands-free, just a few tweaks and suggestions. It could be as simple as getting a band to tour a classic album. Maybe I get them to tighten up and deliver it better. Or maybe I get them to rediscover what was great about themselves. I've just started managing Ocean Colour Scene, and I think my role is to get the band into the zone again. I try to make them feel urgent again by talking to them, underlining their strengths and cutting away the distractions. A long time down the road, a band can lose focus of what they are and what works. Sometimes I change the team around the band. Ocean Colour Scene were caught in the O2 Academy trap of the round of Christmas gigs, and I'm not decrying the Academys but they needed to change what they did. The intention is to take time out and come back bigger and play arenas. Change the impression of the band, make a good new record – a great comeback album.

I like to get up close with my bands. Be on the road with them. Turn up at their gigs. I dip in and out, of course, and I'm not at every gig, but being there when I can – that's how it should be. I want to see the bands. I want to see the gigs and the reaction the bands get and what's going on. You have to be part of the culture. Almost part of the band. I got rid of an agent who never went to see one of the bands they were working for. You have to go to the shows to know what's going on. You just can't blag it. I need to understand what works. I need to spend time with the bands if I can. I need to be part of their world. For me, that's what a manager does.

There are a lot of crossovers between management and running a label. They are dead similar. I think it's good for me to be doing it like this now, though. I manage nine acts, and I've got to be mentally alert to do it right, which is good for my brain. I'll do this until I'm an old guy.

With Oasis I made as much money as I could spend in a lifetime. Despite, or maybe because of that, I got a bit too jaded and comfortable and that wasn't me. So I got out. I had already tried everything. I'd done the sex, drugs and rock 'n' roll, and then I got clean and got into politics, and ran my pal Malcolm McLaren's campaign to become the London mayor, and then I spent years in the country.

I then got Poptones going in 1999, signing bands like The Hives, January, Arnold, Cherrystones, King Biscuit Time, Thee Unstrung, The Boxer Rebellion, Beachbuggy, Pure Reason Revolution and Nick Laird-Clowes as Trashmonk, and then there was my Death Disco club, a weekly indie night in Notting Hill, which was more like a drinking club and which I had no idea was considered a good club. I only realised later on when Eleanor, my friend, said she used to go when she was younger and that it was a brilliant club for hip kids. She said that she loved that club, and I had no idea it was that special because I was pissed all the time! Death Disco really took off, though, and we had branches in

Glasgow, London, New York City, Budapest and Los Angeles. So I must have been doing something right.

If I thought I had escaped the madhouse after I shut Creation down in 1999, I was kidding myself. I came out of the label because, at the end of the day, I had achieved everything I wanted to with it and I was bored. I was trying to get back to me being me, whatever that fucking meant. Sometimes success can make you blind to who you really are. I'd spent a few years trying to find myself but I was missing the action. And I was getting lost. Maybe I was looking for something with a bit more danger. I thought management would be hands off and not as intense as running a label. And maybe it was for most people, but then most people don't end up managing The Libertines.

It was whilst I was doing Death Disco in 2004 that Danny Watson, who DJ'd with me, said that he had heard The Libertines had just broken up with their manager who had got fed up with them. Their label, Rough Trade, was also fed up with them after spending 3 million on the band and still not getting them past headlining the ICA or beyond number 35 in the charts. Then James Endeacott, who had been in the band Loop and was the key A&R in the development of both The Strokes and The Libertines at Rough Trade, rang me up and said, 'We think that you're the guy to manage Pete and Carl.' He asked me three times that summer to do it. I didn't want to but he kept calling. They were asking me to turn it around for Rough Trade because I'm supposedly the don of DIY because I broke Oasis. So I'm now thinking, what can I do?

At the time, things had got very messy with the band. Pete Doherty was trying to do Babyshambles because The Libertines were in a flux. James told me that Peter was in a lot of trouble because he had burgled Carl's house and he was looking at prison. I mean, I was thinking, how is that even illegal? It was his mate's house! Should he go to prison for breaking into his bandmate's house? Lisa Moorish, who was a pal and who I had released on Poptones when she sang for Kill City, took me to see Babyshambles play because she was friends with Pete and had had his daughter Astile in 2003. The gig was utterly shambolic but there was also something great about it.

It was all looking shit but they kept saying, 'Can you talk to Pete?', so I go down to Watford to meet him, and James Endeacott phones me and says 'Where are you?' I took the call because James is my friend and he had asked me to talk to his pop star because Pete doesn't give a fuck about anybody. I had made the journey to meet Pete, and now James seemed to be in disbelief that I was going. He wished me good luck, adding, 'You will need it.' I thought, is he taking the piss? He'd been on at me all summer to meet this cunt and now he's wishing me good luck? I get there and meet Pete and it's even messier than I'd thought. Pete was saying that, basically, he hadn't seen the probation officer for the last three times he was meant to go and he was looking at prison. Now, I don't know much about the law, but I know that if you don't turn up for the probation officer, then it's like an insult to the law and they will send you down if you disrespect the law. I said this to him and he said, 'I don't care.' I said, 'You'll do time and it will be rough because you're a pop star and you'll get raped,' and he still said, 'I don't care.' And he meant it. It was off the scale, an insane conversation.

We ended up in a pub that night. When we got there, Pete said to me, 'Who is your favourite band?' and I said The Beatles, and he tells me to put my five fave tracks on the jukebox. So I put my money in and play 'Hey Jude', 'Hello, Goodbye', 'I Am The Walrus', 'Get Back' and 'Dear Prudence'. After that, I ask him, 'Who is your favourite band?', and he tells me Chas & Dave. For fuck's sake! This was even madder than the stuff before. At that point, he puts five Chas & David records on the jukebox. I thought, for fuck's sake, this nutter is supposed to be saving rock music! That was the first meeting, but despite all that, we got on all right.

The next day I went to America and Pete went to jail for six months. I didn't think too much about it until James Endeacott rang me a few months later and asked me to come to Pete's coming-out-of-jail freedom party. I said ok, I'll go. James proceeded to phone me again and asked that when I came to England, could I have a meeting with the band, and to get rid of the cunts I said I would take the meeting, thinking that would get them off my case. The phone calls were annoying but I took the meeting on the Saturday afternoon at the Landmark Hotel in London.

So I get there and order a bottle of champagne, and even though it's already obvious that I'm drinking in the day, they don't give a fuck that they potentially have an alcoholic manager who is kidding that he is sober but drinking champagne in the afternoon. I then order two more bottles of champagne and by the time the second one has been drunk I'm their manager.

I don't know anything about them but I've signed the hottest rock 'n' roll band in the country. I'm now their manager and I have no plan. I assume that whatever worked for Primals and Oasis will work for them too, so I send Carl and Pete to my big house in Wales. The other bands always loved that shit, getting out to the big house in the country. So I send The Libertines down there to get to know them and make a plan.

It's actually the first day that I'm managing them, and we drive down to Wales and they are actually good value to me but they are not getting on with each other that day.

Or all that week, to be honest. It's a bit moody at my place and Peter is in one end of the house and Carl is in the room next door. The next day I'm up early and I'm speaking to the office and I hear someone coming down the stairs and it's Carl. I look at him in my peripheral vision and I'm instantly stunned. It looks like someone has poured tomato ketchup over his head and he is wearing a spooky mask. His eye is also hanging out of his head. For two seconds I'm in disbelief. 'That's a mask...' I mutter to myself, but when I look I see that his eye is actually really hanging out of his head and dangling on the optic nerve. He mumbled that during the night he had self-harmed after an argument with Pete and head-butted the sink ten times and his eye is now hanging out. I get one of my new baby Charlie's wipes and I put the eye back into his head. I'm now thinking, what the fuck, I only signed this band three days ago and now I got this mad kid holding his eye into his head.

To this day I can't drive, so I phone the farmer at the bottom of the hill and say, 'Help, there's been an accident!' and he drives up and looks surprisingly unphased and takes me and Carl up to Brecon hospital. They have a look and say that he is going to lose his eye and we need to quickly get to Hereford hospital for proper treatment. Eventually, after an hour of holding Carl's eye in with my hand, we finally get there. He's actually still pissed after drinking most of one of

291

those massive bottles of whisky you get at airports, which Pete Doherty's mother had got for the coming-out-of-prison party and they had brought to my house. At Hereford, the surgeon looks at me and then at Carl. I'm a fat older bloke in a tracksuit with a good-looking younger pop star, and he looks at me and says, 'What have you done to your boyfriend?' I say, 'He's not my boyfriend, he's my client!' The doctor looks back in disbelief. They then rush Carl into surgery and pump him full of drugs and he gets his eye stitched back up. Six hours later he comes out of the hospital and they have saved his eye. Of course, typically of The Libertines, it's still not really sorted because they have sewn it the wrong way round. So then I have to take him to Portland Street hospital in London and it costs eight grand to get it done properly.

And that was my first week of managing The Libertines.

EPILOGUE

....

The future beckons

The music biz has got it all wrong. They only look at what's in front of them, but the further away you get from London, the more music means to people and that's reflected in the talent. I think London at this point is a desert for music. I used to think you had to come to London to make music, but now it's towns like Blackburn, Burnley, Huddersfield or Bradford where you can actually see a brilliant new band. These days there is more talent in Stirling than in Shoreditch.

I think that London is just not suited to music. There are a lot of people living on the poverty line in London. It's a hard city to live in. It's so expensive that how can musicians even survive? I've just been to Spain and it's far cheaper to live there. A band can't afford to live in London unless they have rich parents. That affects the kind of people who can even attempt to make music, and that's not good.

I caught a wave in London when I moved there. Someone like me needs to be in the epicentre of shit to make something happen. London is no longer the epicentre. Maybe Los Angeles is now. When I came down to London in 1981 nobody would let you into the scene but we found a way. You could afford to live there then, even if it was in a rundown squat. There was space to exist and then make things happen. That would be impossible now for a working-class kid.

It was so much easier back then. Just after we moved down, we went to Mount Pleasant rehearsal studios in Farringdon. It was me and Innes and a drummer that we had found. We were in one of three rooms. The Gang of Four were in the next room and The Cure in the other and it was mind-blowing. These were the bands that we were aspiring to be like, and there they were right in front of us. That's when I realised that we had made the right move and that we had implanted ourselves in the culture.

Maybe it was because I was an outsider when I was younger that I understood the culture. I don't know. But the more I got involved, the more I caught a wave in London. That was where it was at. By 1981 the punk thing was starting to fade and people were making a new wave of electronic music. That was different to what was going on in The Living Room where I was putting on gigs. Most people in London couldn't be bothered with our scene at first, and then it started to build. We thought we were Wembley Stadium, but it was the back room of a tiny pub and I was bringing in outsider bands like the Nightingales and The Three Johns and The Membranes, and that's where it all started to happen. That was the beginning of the road to Oasis at Knebworth. Would you be able to do that now? Maybe, but it would be a lot harder and maybe you would be better doing it where you came from – the internet means you have a portal and your own media and you are not so isolated, and often the best bands are the ones who come from the outside.

In many ways, it's back to what it was like when I started. There's just me. I don't have any staff or an office and I run the business walking around the streets of London – the city I have come to love. Wherever I am, the business is there as well. It's like the Roman emperors – wherever they were was where the capital was! It's no longer the big operation and the big office that Creation turned into at the end. That sort of dinosaur world is what most people who run record labels are looking for. And fair enough. But that world didn't interest me and it isn't how to run a record label in these times. Despite having been there and done it and then scaling back down, I've never lost the buzz or the excitement of finding new bands, or DJing in small clubs for a hundred quid, or managing the older bands and getting them back into shape. I like going to the gigs and watching the crowd, listening to the band and feeling the noise. Just like I always did. I like to be near the action.

I think pop culture is different too now. There is still great music being made, but its role is less central. It's what you look like that matters now. Social networks like TikTok and Instagram are the pop culture now. Let's not kid ourselves, rock 'n' roll is not about the bands anymore. It's about taking a picture of yourself walking down the street and looking good. I get that. Things change. Things should change. Young kids don't want sad old men telling them what to do anymore. The music is not so important now. It's not about what you're saying. It's not even about the fucking songs, which is sort of appalling. It's totally about what you look like. The vision thing that was always important in rock 'n' roll has become so important that people don't actually need the music, just a great photo for Instagram. That's the vision thing now – it's literally your vision of yourself.

I'm not sure I know how young audiences work anymore. It's different for each generation. The aesthetic of what people are into is so different. Charlie, my daughter, is a punk rocker, but to her it's a different thing than it was to me. This generation are activists and want to change the world. They are way more political than I was, and not as rock 'n' roll. Maybe for us, the music got in the way of changing the world?

When I started it was about who is the next Joy Division. We needed to hear whatever was next and we would wait for the music press or John Peel to find it, or we would run around the cool record shops on a musical mission. The young men then would have long coats on and be talking about deep raincoat feelings. Now it's fucking bands acting like idiots on TikTok so they can go viral.

So where do records and record labels fit into this? Do they even have a purpose anymore? Was Malcolm McLaren right all those years ago when he told me over dinner that rock 'n' roll is for collectors now? It's a different world and maybe we are no longer part of it. Saying that, though, I never thought I'd be any good at social media, but I seem to be. And Liam Gallagher is a genius at it. I couldn't do what Liam does, which is go on Twitter and talk to Joe Smith in Great Yarmouth and have a joke with the guy. It probably takes him a couple of hours a day to reply to people's tweets, and that to me is too much effort. With Instagram, I like the idea that you just put a picture up and go off to meet someone and forget about it. That's the level I'm at.

Maybe my time has passed with young bands. I'm not sure how effective I would be now. I understood my generation.

We were obsessed with rock 'n' roll. I knew what would work, and it worked with the Mary Chain and with Oasis. And even after Oasis it still worked. When I started Poptones I was doing a promo tour in Germany about the new label and I was in the hotel at half one in the morning after doing some media stuff and I was watching some obscure shite indie music show. Suddenly this song called 'I Hate To Say I Told You So' comes on with the full video, and I was like, what the fuck is this? It was completely brilliant. The next day I phoned the office and said find out about The Hives and what record label they are on. The office rang back later and said they were on a small label called Burning Heart and about to get dropped after two albums. Their second album's worldwide sales were about 600 copies. They had fucking bombed. So I approached the record company and gave them five grand and picked up the two albums and said to the band, what I will do is choose the best songs and put them out together as a new album called *Your New Favourite Band* and it really took off.

There were four big hit singles and the album sold over a million copies. All I did was identify what was right about them and get it out there and they became huge.

It was the same with The Libertines. I knew it would work because they had the rock 'n' roll aesthetic. I just knew. Twenty-one-year-olds now are cool as fuck but they relate to things in their own way. As they should. I still work with young bands though, but trying to break them on the scale of my past glories is nowhere near as easy as it once was. The Clockworks are a great band. I found them in a rehearsal room and they are a work in progress. They might be huge but the tail to it is now so long. So far they have put out seven or eight singles and they are still only doing 300 tickets for a gig. Back then, a group like that would be much bigger by now. That's how it is now running a label or managing a band in these times.

Many of the older bands who grew up with physical music don't always get it, whereas I understand that with digital and socials it is more than just records now. With the older bands, I know how to put them in touch with their own music and maybe help them find their direction and work out where their career is going in the modern era. I just move them around a little bit so their natural strengths get to shine and they have a direction to move in. It's on a case-by-case basis, though. Even within each band, it can be very different. With the Happy Mondays, the brothers – Shaun and the late Paul – were very different, and you have to accommodate that and make it work. Now, I let people come to me and then we work out from there what we do. I have a look and a think and then do what's necessary in each individual situation. You can't force yourself on anybody.

If they like you they like you, and if they are not suspicious of what you are doing then even better! I have become very close friends with some bands, yet I've also been managing some people for years who I've barely spoken to, and it can work well either way.

I'm still engaged with music, though. I still really like being in the small clubs – mainly it's with the DJ thing now. I like doing it even if there are no people there. I don't care. I just like playing the music and if it connects with someone then great. Recently I was doing Stone Valley Festival and the promoter paid me a grand to play at four in the afternoon but forgot to tell anyone I was there. I played to about thirty people in the afternoon and then they all left to see someone play a gig, so I ended up playing to a whole field with no people in it and it didn't annoy me, even though it was my first gig after lockdown. I just didn't care. I had the music to listen to and that was enough.

These days the music business is a very efficient bean-counting world that still generates a lot of money but seems unlikely to spark the kinds of cultural revolutions that I so enjoyed. I think the big new indie labels like Domino are brilliant. Laurence Bell, who runs the label, came out of the Fire Records system of keeping everything really tight in order to be successful. These days you have to be really tight with the money. It's no longer as loose as it was. There is not much money in music now, and too many bands and a smaller slice of the cake to fight over. I was a seventies guy living in the eighties and I loved the excess and the madness of that era. I may have done well in the dying days of that world, but Laurence also has done consistently well with the more stripped-down modern system, and he's selling a lot of records with his bands.

I embrace the future by dealing with the past. I think I was the king of analogue. I had worked out how to break bands in an analogue culture. When it went digital I was no longer the king and I had to wear that. In the nineties I fucking knew exactly what to do and how to put that with that and join it together, because I'd had my own little band and label and had learned all the fucking stuff. I learned how to manufacture, make the sleeves, master the records and the production, then the PR, the radio and plugging (if you want to describe plugging as sending a record to John Peel!). I was a child of that period. I then learned about the management side and how bands tour. I did it all. I learned all the nuts and bolts, probably because nobody else wanted to. Now I can't design a poster on the internet, but back in the day I would have had my Letraset out and would lay one out on paper.

I'm still putting out records but I'll be honest, I'm not really looking for something or a new band to break big. But if I see something at random then I'm all in. I don't know why I still put records out as no one seems to be listening to them these days, but I love all the bands the same as I ever did. That never changed. I'm a survivor and and I'm as enthusiastic about the music now as I was then. Maybe I'm back to where I started all those years ago, wandering the streets of London, knocking on doors, only now I run the whole label off my iPhone.

We were never music biz people, but somehow we worked out both the music and the business. Maybe running the label allowed me to become the rock star that the bands I was in didn't. It was certainly creative enough to fill that gap, and it had its own attendant levels of sex and drugs and rock 'n' roll as well. I came into this as a fan, then started a bedroom label and ended up with the biggest band in the world. It was meant to be. In reality, though, we just made the whole thing up as we went along. We didn't follow any rules. Music is the only business where you can do this. Follow your instinct instead of rules. Have no fear.

And there you have it: *that's* how to run a record label.